Books by Erin McHugh:

WHO?

WHAT?

WHERE?

WHEN?

WHY?

WHY?

ERIN MCHUGH

Sterling Publishing Co., Inc.
New York

Library of Congress Cataloging-in-Publication Data Available

10 9 8 7 6 5 4 3 2 1

Published by Sterling Publishing Co., Inc.
387 Park Avenue South, New York, NY 10016
© 2005 by Erin McHugh
Distributed in Canada by Sterling Publishing
^{c}/o Canadian Manda Group, 165 Dufferin Street
Toronto, Ontario, Canada M6K 3H6
Distributed in Great Britain by Chrysalis Books Group PLC
The Chrysalis Building, Bramley Road, London W10 6SP, England
Distributed in Australia by Capricorn Link (Australia) Pty. Ltd.
P.O. Box 704, Windsor, NSW 2756, Australia

Sterling ISBN 1-4027-2573-6

For information about custom editions, special sales, premium and
corporate purchases, please contact Sterling Special Sales
Department at 800-805-5489 or specialsales@sterlingpub.com.

WHY?

BLUE SKIES SMILIN' AT ME

Sunlight passes through the earth's oxygen- and nitrogen-rich atmosphere on its way to the planet's surface. Blue light—one component of the sun's light, which looks white because it is made up of all the colors of the spectrum—has a wavelength that's roughly the size of an atom of oxygen, and so it is continuously redistributed, or scattered, by the oxygen atoms in the atmosphere. The blue light enters our eyes from all sorts of angles, and so we see the sky as blue. (The atmosphere scatters violet light even better, but our eyes are more sensitive to blue.) If the earth had no atmosphere, light would travel directly from the sun to our eyes, and all we would see is bright white light against a black sky. And if the earth's atmosphere contained different gases, we might be looking at a different color of sky.

POINTS OF LIGHT

He may have been gearing up to be first president of the United States, but George Washington lost his battle with Betsy Ross when it came to designing the nation's new flag. Washington wanted a six-pointed star on the new banner, but Ross voted for a five-pointed star, knowing that it would be easier and faster to make. She won, and we have Betsy Ross to thank for the five-pointed stars on the U.S. flag today.

◆

The ice cream company BASKIN-ROBBINS regularly draws from its library of nearly 1,000 recipes to rotate their signature 31 flavors. Why 31? No month in the year has more than 31 days, which means Baskin-Robbins offers a new flavor for every day of the month.

IS IT A HAPPY PUPPY?

Tail wagging is not necessarily the sign of a happy dog. When standing before human beings, dogs will often keep their bodies still, their tails wagging in a rhythmic back-and-forth motion. According to many canine behavioral experts, this combination of body stance and tail motion expresses the internal conflict between dogs' attraction to people and their instinctive caution, suggesting conflict or confusion.

Different tail-wagging and body stance patterns express other emotions: Tail wagging back and forth along with vigorous body movement signals friendly or excited behavior; a tail held high with the tip wagging in jerking movements and a taut, alert torso demonstrate aggression; a low, stiff wagging tail and crouched body represent submission and/or fear.

ORDER IN THE COURT

Oyez is a Middle English word shouted three times in succession in the United States to call a courtroom to order. Pronounced "oh-yay" or "oh-yez," it is derived from the Latin verb *audire*, "to hear," and entered our language—and our court system—through Middle English via Anglo-Norman French. It first appeared in 1425 in English, when French was used as the language of the English courts.

◆

The 1999 JAMES BOND movie *The World Is Not Enough* takes its name from the Bond family motto, *Orbis non sufficit*. The motto appeared in 1969's *On Her Majesty's Secret Service*, where it was seen on a plaque.

A COOLING-OFF PERIOD

One early attempt at air-conditioning worked reasonably well but was too high-maintenance, even for a world leader. In July 1881, President James Garfield, mortally wounded by an assassin's bullet, lay in Washington, D.C.'s sweltering heat (ironically, he was shot in Union Station as he was leaving town to escape the summer's unbearable heat and humidity). In a futile attempt to improve his condition—or at least make him comfortable—naval engineers designed a box to vent cool air, produced by suspending ice-water-saturated cloths in front of a fan, into Garfield's room. Although it did lower the room temperature considerably, it was impractical, and in the two months Garfield lay dying, the early air conditioner used more than half a million pounds of ice.

A modern, more practical air-conditioning system didn't appear until 1906, when Willis Carrier introduced his "apparatus for treating air," which cooled, filtered, and redirected air. Carrier's first system was expensive and often impractical. By 1960, technology had advanced enough to make air-conditioning inexpensive, and it quickly became as important as central heating. Not surprisingly, the 1960s were also the first decade to see more people move into the South than leave since the Civil War.

◆

DOWN AND OUT

The most common reasons for filing for bankruptcy include:
- Extended periods of unemployment
- Large and often unanticipated medical expenses
- Overextended credit
- Marital problems leading to financial hardship

"WITH THIS GARTER . . ."

Brides throw their bouquet to all the single women at a wedding reception, the age-old belief being that the one who catches it will be the next to marry. The removal and tossing of the bride's garter is a slyer and more lascivious reference to the groom's good fortune, and demonstrates a bit of his generous and sharing nature.

ROAD FOOD

Even in the days of Pompeii, people were in a hurry. Or perhaps they lived in small quarters without a kitchen of their own. Believe it or not, early fast-food dining was available down at the corner *thermopolium*, a little neighborhood stand that served hot food and mulled wine from earthenware jars set into a counter. Food could be purchased to go or, in locations with seating, eaten there.

AUTOPILOTS

Though the majority of the world drives on the right-hand side of the road, there are countries where medieval habits die hard. Centuries ago, before the days of motorized transportation, men fought with swords and traveled on horseback. Since most people are right-handed, men would keep their scabbards to their left, drawing—and, if need be, fighting—with the sword in their right hand. Riding on the left side of a road kept their right side, and hand, free for fighting. Today, residents of 166 countries drive on the right side of the road; those in 74 nations (many of which were once colonies of European states) drive on the left.

LINCOLN ASSASSINATION THEORIES

1. Vice President Andrew Johnson—Lincoln's nemesis—was involved with Booth's assassination plan. Allegedly, Johnson received a note written by Booth on the day Lincoln was assassinated.
2. A simple conspiracy, organized by John Wilkes Booth, was responsible for Lincoln's assassination. Booth, a southern patriot and racist, led a small group by himself.
3. Lincoln's assassination was the result of a Confederate plot—the Confederacy's position weakened as the Civil War progressed, and assassination seemed the only resolution. This was a popular theory that arose almost immediately after the president's death.
4. Lincoln's assassination was the result of a conspiracy of powerful international bankers. Not only did the president turn down money from the Rothschilds to finance the war, but they and other European bankers opposed many of his policies, so they hired Booth to kill him.
5. The Roman Catholic Church was behind Lincoln's assassination. The majority of American Catholics were in favor of slavery and opposed to a Lincoln presidency.
6. The secretary of war, Edwin Stanton, was the mastermind behind Lincoln's assassination, as he desired much more stringent Reconstruction policies.

HOW HAPPY?

Why would anyone want to be happy as a clam? The full adage is "Happy as a clam at high tide," and since clams are caught only at low tide—by hand, foot, or rake—it's no wonder these tasty mollusks are indeed happiest at high tide.

WHEN PHIL SPEAKS . . .

Groundhog Day is a distinctly American holiday that arose from the influx to Pennsylvania of German settlers, who brought a Candlemas Day tradition with them to their new country. As far back as the Roman conquest, Germans believed that any animal that cast its shadow on this day signaled six more weeks of winter. With the plethora of groundhogs in the Keystone State, they—and Punxsutawney Phil in particular—got the job. Back in Europe, there was even an old English song:

> If Candlemas be fair and bright,
> Come, winter, have another flight;
> If Candlemas brings clouds and rain,
> Go winter, and come not again.

THE NOT-SO-WORLDLY SERIES

Legend has it that the World Series got its name from the *New York World*, a newspaper that was said to have sponsored early baseball championship games. But it's not true; the *World* never played such a role. By 1886, the postseason contest was called the World's Championship (and so cited in *Spalding's Base Ball Guide* for 1887), since both American and National League winners wished to call themselves "America's Champions"; it was assumed that teams from other countries would one day enter the contest. By the time of the Red Sox–Pirates series in 1903, the playoffs were referred to as the World Championship Series, eventually shortened to World Series. To this day, only U.S. and Canadian teams have competed in the World Series.

LIGHT SHOW

The aurora borealis, or northern lights, and the aurora australis, or southern lights, are the heavenly result of the interaction between the solar wind and earth's magnetic field. The sun emits highly charged particles, or ions, that speed through space, forming a cloud of ions called plasma. The stream of plasma coming from the sun is called solar wind. When plasma hits the earth's magnetic field, some of the ions become trapped by the earth's magnetic forces and follow magnetic lines into the ionosphere (more than 30 miles above the earth's surface), where they collide with various atmospheric gases, mostly oxygen and nitrogen, generating up to 1 million megawatts of electricity and the characteristic sky glow. Generally red, green, blue, and violet in color, the aurora appears in a variety of forms, from simple patches of light to streamers, arcs, banks, rays, and curtains.

COME 'N' GET IT

Why do mosquitoes seem to zoom in on some people while completely ignoring others? Mosquitoes have a complex set of sensors that lead them to human prey from as far as 100 feet away. These sensors can detect chemicals that both mammals and birds emit, including those in sweat. Mosquitoes can also detect movement, and they assume anything moving is alive and therefore full of blood. They can also detect heat and can find warm-blooded mammals at close range. All in all, avoiding mosquitoes might just be a losing battle.

◆

Our present-day usage of the word ALIBI has never changed from the Latin: it is an adverb meaning "elsewhere."

VERY SLIPPERY

Scientists used to think that ice was slippery because the pressure exerted on it from a skate, puck, or even a pair of galoshes created friction, and the resultant heat melted a thin top layer of ice. But by examining ice crystals up close, they've discovered that the molecules on the surface of the ice vibrate more than usual for a solid—though they vibrate only up and down, not in all directions, as would be the case in a liquid. The result is a quasi-fluid layer on the top of the ice, making slipping and sliding practically inevitable.

THE GREAT WAR

In 1918, the Committee for Public Information, an office of the United States government whose purpose was to elicit support for World War I, published a set of official reasons why America opted to enter the war. They were:

1. Germany's continued submarine warfare
2. Imperial Germany becoming an international outlaw
3. Prussian militancy and autocracy disturbing the balance of world power and international equilibrium
4. Autocratic nations threatening world democracy
5. Isolationism no longer being a viable option in an age of growing global interdependence
6. The threat to America's independence

◆

It is not likely that you will sink in QUICKSAND unless you dive in headfirst. Your body is less dense than the quicksand; if you relax, you will eventually float to the top, as you would in water.

OW! HA HA

Not so funny, the funny bone. Frankly, it hurts when you hit it. It's not a bone, of course—it's the ulnar nerve, which runs down the length of the arm. It lies close to the skin's surface, and since most of us have very little fat for cushioning at the back of the elbow, when that spot is struck just right, the ulnar nerve presses into the humerus, which is the long bone that runs from your elbow to shoulder. The result is a tingling sensation that runs down the ulnar nerve through your forearm and into your ring and little fingers.

RAINING CATS

Cats are said to have nine lives because they are rarely injured when they fall. Some veterinarians believe that the longer a cat's fall, the better chance it has for survival. Cats have a finely tuned sense of balance in their inner ears, their whiskers are highly sensitive to surrounding vibrations, they use all four feet evenly to cushion a fall (they bend their knees on impact, too), and they instinctively spread their limbs like a feline umbrella, which slows their fall considerably. All of these advantages add up to at least nine happy lives!

FOR WHOM DOES THE BELL TOLL?

It tolls for Sir Benjamin Hall. Big Ben is not the clock atop London's House of Parliament, but the thirteen-and-a-half-ton bell inside the clock tower. Cast in 1858, its installation was directed by Sir Benjamin, who was the commissioner of works at the time. The moniker was probably coined by the *Times* (not by Sir Benjamin as an act of self-promotion).

MOUNTIES' MISSION

In 1873, the Canadian government established the North-West Mounted Police—the forerunner of the Royal Canadian Royal Mounted Police—to form law enforcement detachments throughout the prairies and establish friendly relations with the native population (now known as the First Nations), contain the whiskey trade and enforce prohibition, supervise treaties between the First Nations and the federal government, assist the settlement process by ensuring the welfare of immigrants, and fighting prairie fires, disease, and destitution. The first detachment left Dufferin, Manitoba, on July 8, 1874, and arrived in southern Alberta in October. The detachment included about 275 officers and men, 142 draft oxen, 93 head of cattle, 310 horses, 114 Red River carts, 73 wagons, a pair of nine-pounder field guns, a couple of mortars, mowing machines, portable forges, and field kitchens.

"HERE, HORSEY . . ."

The reason firehouses have circular stairways dates back to the days when fire engines were pulled by horses. Horses were stabled on the ground floor but occasionally got out of their stalls. The curved stairs prevented them from getting onto the upper floor.

◆

Only three of the 263 previous POPES have been called "the Great"—Pope Leo I, Pope Nicholas I, and Pope Gregory I. The "Great" title is merely bestowed as a popular acclamation by the people and is not any sort of official title.

VIGILANTE JUSTICE

The term *lynching*—to put to death without legal sanction—
comes from Captain William Lynch (1742–1820), a man who,
along with his neighbors, decided to rid Pittsylvania County,
Virginia, of bands of thieves. Edgar Allan Poe reported that
Captain Lynch and his "lynch men" had drawn up an agree-
ment, dated September 22, 1780, that read, "If they will not
desist from their evil practices, we will inflict such corporal
punishment on him or them, as to us shall seem adequate to
the crime committed or the damage sustained."

Lynch and many others felt that large Virginia cities and
their courts were too far away (nearly 150 miles from Rich-
mond) for swift and reasonable justice, especially when
crimes of violence had been committed. They considered
lynching, along with other forms of frontier punishment,
appropriate and necessary, declaring that they were "aiding
the civil authority."

JUST A MIRAGE

Seeing things? When light passes through two layers of air
with different temperatures, you may see a mirage. It's especially common in the desert—sun heats the sand, which in
turn heats the air just above it. The hot air bends light rays,
and so when you think you're seeing a lake, what you're
really looking at is a reflection of the sky above.

GOOD DOG

Fido may be a favorite puppy name dating from Roman
times: it comes from the Latin *fidus*, meaning "faithful."

SPLITSVILLE

Over half of all marriages don't last. Here are the most common reasons, according to several surveys, married couples split:

- Lack of commitment to the marriage
- Dramatic change in priorities
- Couple's marital satisfaction decreases
- Desertion
- Bigamy
- Personal safety and protection of children
- Imprisonment
- Institutionalization
- Poor communication
- Financial problems
- Irretrievable breakdown of some kind
- Chronic abuse—sexual or physical
- Chronic substance abuse
- Sexual infidelity
- Betrayed trust
- Falling in love with another person

HOW DOES IT KNOW?

DuPont's nonstick Teflon seems to be a conundrum: If it's a nonadhesive surface, how do they get it to stick to the pan? Teflon won't chemically bond to anything except itself, but it can be forced into nooks and crannies. The metal surface of the pan is roughened, and then a primer is applied; the Teflon is embedded in the primer, and then additional layers of Teflon are applied on top of that.

SLEEP ON IT

The phrase "You made your bed—now lie in it" is more lit-eral than one could imagine. Centuries ago, as soon as spring came, people took their mattresses outside, slit them open, and aired out the straw, horsehair, and whatever else they had used to stuff the mattress. But after the long winter (and given what passed for cleanliness at the time), it was not unusual to find mites, bedbugs, mice, and all manner of sur-prises inside. The job was to clean out the stuffing and restuff the mattress—and however well or poorly you did the job, you had to sleep on it, hence the saying.

THE PURPLE HEART

The Purple Heart is the oldest military decoration for the common soldier still in use in the world, and the first American award made available to common soldiers. When the Continental Congress told General George Washington there was no money for new commissions, he designed a new badge of honor: "Whenever any singularly meritorious action is performed, the author of it shall be permitted to wear on his facings, over his left breast, the figure of a heart in purple cloth or silk edged with narrow lace or binding. Not only instances of unusual gallantry but also of extraordi-nary fidelity and essential service in any way shall meet with due reward."

Today the Purple Heart is awarded to members of the U.S. armed forces who are wounded by an instrument of war in the hands of the enemy, and posthumously to the next of kin for those killed in action or who die of wounds received in action. It is specifically a combat decoration.

FIFTY WAYS TO NAME YOUR COUNTRY

The Origins of Each of the United States

Alabama: Believed to come from two Choctaw words, *alba*, meaning "vegetation" or "plants," and *amo*, "gatherer."

Alaska: Derived from the Aleut word *alyeska*, meaning "great land" or "that which the sea breaks against."

Arizona: A combination of Indian words *aleh* and *zon*, meaning "little spring."

Arkansas: Ohio Valley Indians referred to the local Quapaw Indians as the Arkansas, or "south wind."

California: A mythical Spanish island, ruled by a queen named Califia, which appeared in a Spanish romance (c. 1500) called *Las Sergas de Esplandián*.

Colorado: From the Spanish word for "colored."

Connecticut: From the Indian name Quinnehtukqut, which means "beside the long tidal river."

Delaware: Named after Delaware River and Delaware Bay, which were named for Sir Thomas West, Baron de la Warr.

District of Columbia: Built on land known as the Territory of Columbia.

Florida: From the Spanish festival day Pascua de Florida, or "feast of flowers," referring to Easter.

Georgia: Named in honor of George II of England.

Hawaii: Origin uncertain, but one theory has it that the name comes from Hawaii Loa, who in traditional lore discovered the islands, or it may be named after the legendary ancestral home of the Polynesian people.

Idaho: An invented word from an unknown source.

Illinois: Algonquin for "tribe of superior men."

Indiana: Meaning "land of Indians," the name was given to the Indiana Territory by the U.S. Congress when Indiana was created from the Northwest Territory.

Iowa: The tribal name of the Iowa Indians, Ayuxwa, was spelled *Ioway* by the English and means "this is the place" or "beautiful land."

Kansas: From the Sioux *kanze*, meaning "south wind."

Kentucky: From the Iroquois word *ken-tah-ten*, meaning "land of tomorrow."

Louisiana: The area was named La Louisiane after Louis XIV of France.

Maine: So named to distinguish the mainland from the off-shore islands; also thought to be a compliment to Henrietta Maria, wife of Charles I and queen of England, who owned the province of Mayne in France.

Maryland: For King Charles's wife, Queen Henrietta Maria.

Massachusetts: Opinions differ, but the most popular theory is that it's a combination of the Indian words *massa*, "great," and *wachusett*, "mountain-place."

Michigan: Derived from the Chippewa word *majigan*, referring to a clearing on the lower peninsula.

Minnesota: From the Dakota word *mnishota*, meaning "cloudy water."

Mississippi: From the Chippewa word meaning "father of waters."

Missouri: Named after the local Sioux tribe, meaning "he of the large canoes."

Montana: Derived from the Latin word *montaanus*, "mountainous."

Nebraska: From an Oto word meaning "flat water."

Nevada: Spanish sailors originally called the California mountains the Sierra Nevada, meaning "snowcapped range"; the name of this new territory was a shorter version, meaning simply "snowcapped."

New Hampshire: Captain John Mason named the land he had been granted after the English county he had lived in as a child.

New Jersey: After the Channel isle of Jersey.

New Mexico: Named after Mexitli, an Aztec god.

New York: Named by the British to honor the Duke of York.

North Carolina: Named in honor of Charles I of England.

North Dakota: From the Sioux word for "friend."

Ohio: From the Iroquois word meaning "great river."

Oklahoma: A combination of two Choctaw words, *ukla*, "person," and *humá*, "red."

Oregon: The origin is in question, although the Columbia River, along the state's northern border, was called the Ouragan, which is French for "hurricane"; others believe the name arose from a mapmaker's error in the 1700s.

Pennsylvania: "Penn's woods," after William Penn.

Rhode Island: Either from the Greek island of Rhodes or from the Dutch *roodt eylandt*, "red island," for the red clay along the shore.

South Carolina: Like North Carolina, named in honor of Charles I of England.

South Dakota: Like North Dakota, from the Sioux word for "friend" (the two states were one territory until 1899).

Tennessee: From the Tennessee River, which took its name from Tanasi, two Cherokee villages on its banks.

Texas: From the Caddo word *teysha*, meaning "hello, friend."

Utah: *Yuttahih*, an Apache name for the Ute tribe, means "people of the mountains."

Vermont: Anglicized version of French explorer Samuel de Champlain's choice *Vert Mont*, meaning "green mountain."

Virginia: For Elizabeth I of England, the "Virgin Queen."

Washington: The Washington Territory, established in 1853, was named for President George Washington.

West Virginia: Like Virginia (West Virginia was not a separate state until 1861), named in honor of Queen Elizabeth I.

Wisconsin: From the French version of the Chippewa word for "grassy place" or "gathering of the waters."

Wyoming: From the Delaware Indian word, meaning "mountains and valleys alternating" (the Delawares lived much farther east, but the name is taken from the Wyoming Valley in Pennsylvania).

PLACE NAMES FROM AROUND THE WORLD

Argentina: From the Latin *argentum,* "silver."

Barbados: The term *os barbados* means "the bearded ones" in Portuguese, a reference to the island's fig trees, whose long roots resemble beards.

Brazil: From the native brazilwood tree, named because its wood was the color of red-hot embers (*brasil* in Portuguese).

Britain: From Pritani, a Celtic tribe mentioned as early as the first century B.C.E. by Diodorus Siculus as the island's original inhabitants.

Canada: *K'anata* meant "little settlement" to the Algonquins, and referred to Stadacona, a village near what is now Quebec City.

Christmas Island: Discovered by Captain William Mynors on Christmas Day in 1643.

Costa Rica: Spanish for "rich coast," so named because Christopher Columbus thought there was gold there.

Cyprus: Named for the copper (Greek *kypros*) that was found on the island.

Ethiopia: From the Latin *Aethiopia,* meaning "land of burned faces."

Gambia: Probably from the Portuguese *câmbio,* meaning "trade"; the Portuguese monopolized trade there in the sixteenth century.

Hong Kong: In Cantonese, *heung gong* means "fragrant harbor" or "spice harbor."

Hungary: From the Turkic *on-ogur,* for "people of the ten spears," after the seven Magyar tribes and three Khazar tribes who settled there.

Israel: From the Genesis story; an alternative Hebrew name for Jacob, meaning "he struggles with God."

Japan: English pronunciation for the Chinese for "land of the rising sun," a reminder that the country is east of China.

Kenya: After the Kikuyu people's *kirinyaga,* the "mountain of whiteness," referring to Mount Kenya; the British mispronounced it as "Kenya."

Kyrgyzstan: Derives from three Persian words meaning "land of forty tribes."

Luxembourg: From *lucilemburrugh,* a combination of Celtic and German words meaning "little castle."

Malta: Most likely derived from the Latin *melitta,* "honey," which was the island's major export during classical times.

Mongolia: First used by the Chinese, meaning "brave" or "fearless."

Namibia: From the Nama language, referring to the Namib Desert (*namib* means "enormous").

Nepal: Means "wool market" in Tibetan.

Pakistan: An acronym created by Muslim nationalist Choudhary Rahmat Ali in 1933:

P	Punjab
A	Afghania
K	Kashmir
S	Sindh
TAN	Balochistan

The *I* was added for ease of pronunciation. However, in his 1947 book *Pakistan: the Fatherland of the Pak Nation*, Ali modified his own acronym:

P	Punjab
A	Afghania
K	Kashmir
I	Iran
S	Sindh
T	Turkharistan
A	Afghanistan
N	Balochistan

Papua New Guinea: The neighboring Malays, who have straight hair, called the natives *papua*, "frizzy hair."

Sudan: From the Arabic for "land of the blacks."

Ukraine: From *krajina*, a Slavic term for "border territory."

Uruguay: From a Guarani word meaning "river of shellfish."

Vatican City: From *Mons Vaticanus*, the Roman hill on which the Papal palace stands.

Viet Nam: From a Chinese term meaning "beyond the southern border."

♦

SO ROMANTIC

Don Juan came up with the cocktail-party phrase "breaking the ice." At least that's the derivation based on Lord Byron's description of the British in his famous 1821 poem "Don Juan": "And your cold people are beyond all price, / When once you've broken through their confounded ice."

AVAST!

What ho? Could it be that Moby-Dick did indeed live and breathe? There had long been a story about an actual white whale told by whalers who sailed the Pacific Ocean, and an article written by Jeremiah Reynolds and published in 1839 in *The Knickerbocker* told the tale. Captain Nathaniel Palmer, while aboard the whaler *Penguin*, told of his victory battling a leviathan known as Mocha Dick, which was often spotted in the waters near the Mocha Islands off Chili. Herman Melville's novel did not appear until 1851, but Reynolds's description has a strangely familiar sound: "From the effect of age, or more probably from a freak of nature, as exhibited in the case of the Ethiopian Albino, a singular consequence had resulted—*he was white as wool!*"

COCKROACH VS. HUMAN

For millions of years, humankind has lost the fight against cockroaches; there are plenty of reasons. A cockroach can:

- Be frozen for two days and still survive
- Go three months without any food at all
- Live a week without its head
- Hold its breath up to forty minutes
- Be as much as six inches long with a one-foot wingspan
- Live through a thermonuclear explosion
- Navigate perfectly if both deaf and blind

Our word INCH comes form the Latin *uncia*, meaning "a twelfth part."

SHIVER ME TIMBERS!

Goose bumps (so named because they make a person look like a plucked goose) are a signal from the hypothalamus, the body's thermostat, that we need to warm ourselves. It's part of the shivering reflex, in which the body's muscles and glands begin working to heat up the body. This reflex is involuntary, contracting and relaxing the skeletal muscles; the hair on your body pulls up and the ducts to the sweat glands contract, conserving heat. The entire body can go to work in an extreme situation: every muscle in the body, except those in the eyeballs, can shiver—even the tongue.

SOME LIKE IT HOT

Crickets make a variety of chirping sounds, called stridulation (males are the "singers"), for a variety of reasons:

- A loud, monotonous sound to attract a female
- A quick, soft chirp to court and impress a female
- An aggressive sound to warn male intruders away from his territory

This language, spoken by scraping one wing against another, is simply a variation of courtship and survival that is often observed in the animal kingdom. But the cricket offers a singular service to humans that no one else in nature seems to have mastered: They tell the temperature. To get a rough idea of what to wear and how to prepare for a picnic or outdoor concert, check your watch and count the number of chirps you hear in fifteen seconds. Add 37 to that number, and you'll have the approximate temperature in degrees Fahrenheit.

THE GRIM REAPER
The American Medical Association's List of the Major Causes of Death in the United States (as of 2000)

Tobacco (smoking)	435,000
Poor diet and physical inactivity	365,000
Alcohol (includes alcohol-related motor vehicle deaths)	85,000
Microbial agents	75,000
Toxic agents	55,000
Adverse reactions to prescription drugs	32,000
Suicide	30,622
Incidents involving firearms	29,000
Motor vehicle crashes	26,347
Homicide	20,308
Illicit drug use, direct and indirect	17,000
Anti-inflammatory drugs such as aspirin	7,600

HAIL, SPARKY!

Dalmatians enjoyed a long and illustrious career before catching the imagination of Walt Disney. Centuries ago they were known as "coach dogs" and ran alongside stagecoaches, guarding against marauders and highwaymen. When horse-drawn fire engines came into use, dalmatians were used because they bonded with horses and were easily trained to run ahead of them and clear streets quickly in emergencies.

◆

For centuries people believed that the VEIN in the fourth finger of one's left hand went directly to the heart, which is why wedding rings are traditionally worn there.

SHALL WE DANCE?

The Whirling Dervishes are Sufis who trace their origin to the thirteenth-century Ottoman Empire. The dervish's dance is a mystical exercise, part of a sacred ceremony. The dervish spins in a precise rhythm, emptying himself of all thought in order to enter a trancelike state.

During the ritual dance, or *sema*, there are four *selams*, or musical movements, each with a distinct rhythm. The first *selam* represents the human being's birth to truth through feeling and mind. The second *selam* expresses the rapture of the human being witnessing the splendor of creation in the face of God's greatness and omnipotence. The third *selam* is the rapture of dissolving into love and the sacrifice of the mind to love. In the fourth *selam* the dervish, after the ascent of his spiritual journey, returns to his task, servanthood to God.

ROADSIDE AMERICA

Miniature golf was first introduced in 1916 with a course designed by James Barber in Pinehurst, North Carolina (legend has it that when Barber saw the finished course, he declared, "This'll do!"—providing the course with its name, Thistle Dhu). It became particularly popular during the Depression, as a round of miniature golf cost less than seeing a movie; also, in a decade seemingly gone haywire, it offered a place where the world was brought down to a manageable size. It became one of America's first roadside franchises in the 1930s and 1940s, and the industry grew even as other businesses failed. By midcentury, miniature golf was enjoying a pint-sized form of the suburban sprawl taking place in much of the United States.

CRAZY CAT

Catnip (*Nepeta cataria*) is a common herb in the mint family that grows easily in any garden. Nepetalactone is the secret ingredient that makes cats crazy, and it's recently been found to repel cockroaches and the mosquitoes that carry yellow fever. Herbalists recommend catnip for human use as a treatment for colic, headache, fever, toothache, colds, and spasms. It is also an excellent sleep inducer (try a cup of catnip tea).

But back to the cats. About 30 percent of the feline population—including most tiny kittens and old cats—do not respond to catnip at all. Reaction from interested cats lasts only five to fifteen minutes; once the cat acclimates to the catnip, it loses interest for an hour or more, at which point the cycle starts over again.

CATNIP BEHAVIOR

1. Sniffing
2. Licking and chewing the toy or plant, head shaking
3. Chin and cheek rubbing
4. Rolling and body rubbing
5. Grasping and kicking

SHAZAM!

The term *hanky-panky* was not originally used to connote sexual hijinks, as one might think, but is instead a magician's term from the 1800s. Prestidigitators used to wave handkerchiefs to distract the audience from whatever trick they were performing with their other hand. Like the rhyming *hocus-pocus*, which was already in use, *hanky-panky* became a catchphrase for anything suspicious or sneaky, like a little romance on the side.

THE PSYCHOLOGY OF COLOR

Color is never just about the way it looks, whether it's on your back or on your walls; it's about how it makes you feel, and the message it sends about you to others. Much research has been done on meaning of color—how it affects people's lives, their temperaments, and even their buying habits.

Red: This color represents fire, passion, warmth, heat, and love; power, excitement, and aggression. It's no wonder it can elevate blood pressure, quicken breathing, and cause people to make snap decisions. Red is known to be an appetite stimulant, though an entire room of scarlet will make one anxious. Bars, casinos, and restaurants often use scarlet accents in the hope that it will, as experts say, help people lose track of time.

Orange: The hue most associated with appetite, orange is almost universally appealing, and is wholesome and warm. Orange is often used in packaging to make an expensive product appear more affordable.

Yellow: The most visible of all the colors, yellow is the top attention getter; since it enhances concentration, it has become the color of choice for legal pads and Post-Its. Yellow speeds up the metabolism and is the most fatiguing color to the eye.

Green: This shade is the most popular for decorating. It's soothing to the mind and eye and is familiar and calming, because it's seen so much in nature. Not only is it easy on the senses, but experts say it can actually improve vision. Hospitals and other institutions rely on its peaceful and relaxing qualities.

Blue: Blue causes the body to produce chemicals that relax the nervous system. Research has proven that people are more productive in blue rooms—students test better, and weight lifters lift more. Both men and women most favor blue, and retain more information when the text is blue.

Purple: Magisterial, luxurious, and sophisticated, this color can evoke passion and romance. However, because it is so rarely found in nature, it can easily appear artificial.

Brown: Brown is solid, earthy, and reliable, and men are apt to cite it as one of their favorite colors. Its solidity and strength promote comfort and openness.

Pink: Less in-your-face than its scarlet counterpart, people find it romantic and tender. It can be calming (some go so far as to say tranquilizing) when in a room, causing visitors to be soft-hearted.

Though black and white are technically not colors, as they don't appear in the spectrum, their place in color psychology is as important as all the others:

Black: Priests wear black to signify their submission to God, and other people wear it to connote formality. Color psychologists consider it the most controversial of colors: it's associated with both witches and demons, sturdiness and reliability. Black is not a true color—in pigmentation, it's the presence of all color; in light, it's the absence.

White: This color symbolizes innocence and purity. Doctors and nurses wear it to imply a sterile environment. White pigmentation is the absence of any color; white light indicates the presence of all colors.

TAPHOPHOBIA

Psychologists tell us that taphophobia—the fear of being buried alive—is very common. Some famous examples:

> "All I desire for my own burial is not to be buried alive."
> —LORD CHESTERFIELD

> "Have me decently buried, but do not let my body be put into a vault in less than two days after I am dead."
> —GEORGE WASHINGTON

Prior to the advent of embalming, being buried alive was a common fear—though a rare occurrence. The eighteenth century brought about the invention of the signaling, or escape hatch, coffin. There were several types of these coffins, but they all had in common a mechanism that allowed communication from the buried person to the world above. Some of the accoutrements of these rigged-up coffins included firecrackers, bells, flags, and breathing tubes—one version even provided a shovel, food, and water. The fad didn't last long, however, and the signaling coffin soon disappeared. But not the fear of being buried alive: a patent for a "coffin alarm" was applied for as recently as 1983.

◆

MEXICAN JUMPING BEANS are real, all right—they even have a Latin name: *Laspeyresia saltitans*. However, they're not beans at all, but moth larvae, which grow inside the seed capsules of a Mexican desert shrub. The larvae roll around inside the seed capsule when they detect warmth and light, causing the seed capsule to "jump." After three to five months, these larvae spin a cocoon, and a small number of them hatch as moths, living only a few days.

COLOR ME ASLEEP

Dreaming in color is one thing, but what about dreaming in particular colors? What do colors in dreams mean?

Colors	Representation
Beige	The basics, neutrality
Black	The unknown, danger, death, hate
Black and white	Need for more objectivity in making decisions
Blue	Truth, justice, heaven, tranquility
Brown	Practicality, domestic comfort, the earth
Burgundy	Wealth, success, the potential for power
Fuchsia	Spirituality, meditation, emotional stability
Gold	Spiritual rewards, richness, refinement
Gray	Fear, depression, ill health
Green	Growth, hope, healing, peace, wealth; jealousy
Hot pink	Sex, lust
Ivory	Slightly tainted purity
Maroon	Courage, strength
Orange	Friendliness, warmth, courtesy
Peach	Innocent love
Pink	Love, joy, sweetness
Purple	Devotion, compassion
Red	Intense passion, power, anger, courage; also shame, sexual impulses
Silver	Justice and purity
Teal	Trustworthiness, devotion
Turquoise	Healing power, natural energy
Violet	Religious aspiration, purification
White	Purity, peace, innocence, new beginnings
Yellow	In a positive dream, energy, harmony, optimism; in a negative dream, cowardice and sickness

SCHOOL UNIFORMS

The wearing of caps and gowns for graduation is the last vestige of a long tradition of both keeping vows and keeping warm. When European universities developed in the twelfth century, teachers and students alike began to wear long gowns. Gowns were standard clerical garb, and scholars of the day took a type of minor vow with the Church. As university connections to the Church began to dissipate, the gowns stayed, providing warmth to students and faculty who lived and taught in the cold, drafty buildings. Gowns are still de rigueur in many universities throughout the world, but they are worn for ceremonial use only in the United States, though their design is regulated. The shape of the sleeve and hood show the degree a student has pursued: a bachelor's gown has no hood and pointed sleeves, the master's has closed sleeves with arm slits and a narrow hood; the doctor's has bell sleeves and a draped, wide hood. The hood's lining denotes the college. And as for caps, velvet is worn by doctors only, please.

HEAVY STUFF

The materials that go into making an airplane's flight information data recorder—the "black box"—include stainless steel and high-temperature insulation, which surround a locator beacon and memory unit. If you've ever wondered why an entire plane isn't made out of the black box material, since they always seem to make it through a crash without substantial damage, it's simply that it would be too heavy: the plane would never get off the ground. And by the way, the black box is painted orange.

SO FUNNY I FORGOT TO LAUGH

"Why did the chicken cross the road?" is perhaps the best-known example of what is called anti-humor, a strangely twisted brand of comedy that relies on irony for a humorous response. The listener expects a punch line to be obvious, and when the answer is nonsensical, this seems funny.

Oh, the answer? "To see his friend Gregory Peck."

THE TWELVE LINKS OF DEPENDENT ORIGINATION

Buddhism teaches the ultimate elaboration of the principles of cause and effect, or conditions, which explain the concept of the interdependency of existence.

1. Ignorance is the condition for mental formation.
2. Mental formation is the condition for consciousness.
3. Consciousness is the condition for name and form.
4. Name and form are the condition for the six senses.
5. The six senses are the condition for contact.
6. Contact is the condition for feeling.
7. Feeling is the condition for craving.
8. Craving is the condition for clinging.
9. Clinging is the condition for becoming.
10. Becoming is the condition for birth.
11. Birth is the condition for aging and death.
12. Aging and death are the condition for ignorance.

◆

Israeli POSTAGE STAMPS are special: the glue on the back is certified kosher.

MOVING RIGHT ALONG

History repeats itself in myriad ways, and people's reasons for emigrating have not changed much over time, according to experts at the Ellis Island Immigration Museum:

> Religious or ethnic persecution
> Natural disaster
> Famine
> Homeland economic problems
> War (or fear of war)
> Feudalism and its overthrow
> Political strife
> No son to provide economic protection for the
>   parents in later life
> Oppression
> Following family and friends
> Adoption
> Slavery
> Criminal incarceration
> Being deported

DRINK UP

Alcohol does not kill brain cells but rather damages dendrites—the branched ends of nerve cells that serve as electrical connections to the cells. Losing function of these ends means cutting off incoming messages, which disrupts brain function. Thankfully, most of this damage is not permanent. But that's nothing—back in the day, promoters of temperance also claimed that excessive amounts of alcohol in the blood could cause one to easily catch fire and burn alive.

MONEY FOR NOTHING?

Here are the ten most common reasons grant applications for funding from philanthropic organizations and agencies are declined:

1. "The organization does not meet our priorities."
2. "The organization is not located in our geographic area of funding."
3. "The proposal does not follow our prescribed format."
4. "The proposal is poorly written and difficult to understand."
5. "The proposed budget and grant request are not within our funding range."
6. "We don't know these people—are they credible?"
7. "The proposal doesn't seem urgent—and I'm not sure it will have an impact."
8. "The objectives and plan of action of the project greatly exceed the budget and timelines for implementation."
9. "We've allocated all the money for this grant cycle."
10. "There is insufficient evidence that the program will become self-sufficient and sustain itself after the grant is completed."

(Source: Grant Guides Plus, Inc.)

A LITTLE SOMETHING ON THE SIDE

Before it was food, it was a building. The literal meaning of the French phrase *hors d'oeuvre* was an outbuilding that was not part of the main architectural design. The culinary community borrowed it to describe an appetizer served apart from the main course.

ROOM AT THE INN

America was booming by the 1820s, and the number of travelers—transients, businessmen, even vacationers—was increasing dramatically. To serve them, a new type of hostelry was born. The hotels that sprang up in the center of towns offered meeting rooms, fine restaurants, and a variety of other creature comforts. The most American touch of all? The best lodgings were no longer reserved for guests with impressive titles, as they had been in Europe. Only money got you top-of-the-line service.

WASH ME CLEAN

You washed your hands. Then you washed your dog's dirty paws. So why isn't that bar of soap dirty?

Soap is made from a compound with two components, one hydrophobic (water-insoluble), the other hydrophilic (water-soluble). The former attaches itself to dirt and dissolves it, while the latter keeps the dirty, greasy stuff that was just on your clothes or hands suspended in water, ready to wash away.

As for when hands are really clean: an old wives' tale proposes that to make sure children wash their hands extremely well, they should sing their ABCs. It takes approximately fifteen seconds, the amount of time suggested for a good, germ-ridding scrub.

◆

The OPOSSUM has changed so little since the Cretaceous period, when dinosaurs still roamed the earth, that it's often referred to as a living fossil.

THE DANGERS OF MARRIAGE

The nuances of a wedding are mired in custom and fraught with superstition, and even the days of the week and months in when one marries were thought to carry their own special connection to the couple's ultimate success.

Monday for wealth
Tuesday for health
Wednesday the best day of all
Thursday for losses
Friday for crosses
Saturday for no luck at all.

Advice on the month is even more specific:

Married when the year is new, he'll be loving, kind, and true.
When February birds do mate, you wed nor dread your fate.
If you wed when March winds blow, joy and
sorrow both you'll know.
Marry in April when you can, joy for maiden and for man.
Marry in the month of May, and you'll surely rue the day.
Marry when June roses grow, over land and sea you'll go.
Those who in July do wed, must labor for their daily bread.
Whoever wed in August be, many a change is sure to see.
Marry in September's shrine, your living will
be rich and fine.
If in October you do marry, love will come but riches tarry.
If you wed in bleak November, only joys
will come, remember.
When December snows fall fast,
marry and true love will last.

POINT IN QUESTION

The question mark probably first appeared in the ninth century, though a point or dot at the end of a sentence had long been used to show a full stop. For a query it was followed by a curved line tilted upward to the right. This indicated the cadence and intonation of the voice of the speaker.

WELCOME CHAOS

Who says chaos theory has nothing to do with real life? For over a decade, washing machine manufacturers have been selling a consumer product that exploits randomness. The washing machine maker added a second tiny pulsator to stir the water; it relies on predictable movements while working in a nonlinear way, the basis of chaos theory. Results? The clothes come out cleaner and less tangled.

THE SMELL OF VICTORY, AND THEN SOME

Perfume has a long history as more than a come-on. The Greeks used scents for medicinal purposes—for example, rose petals were worn around the neck to ward off hangovers. Both the Romans and the Crusaders put perfume on before battle, believing that it brought good luck. And Nero had an obsession with beautiful odors—his first-century palace had pipes hidden throughout to spray his guests with rich scents.

◆

Scientists believe that OCTOPI, like humans, turn red when angry and blanch white when afraid.

WHY DIE?

Suicide prevention organizations list these as the leading reasons people attempt and/or commit suicide:

Depression
Schizophrenia, personality disorder, etc.
Alcoholism and substance abuse
Illness and physical infirmity
Revenge, anger, punishment
Sacrifice for others or the community
Politics
Suicide bombers
Loss of a loved one
Loss of job, economic distress
Sexual orientation, gender conflicts

WHAT FLOATS YOUR BOAT?

It's about buoyancy, the upward force a fluid exerts on an object less dense than itself—that's what allows even gigantic things to float in liquid. An object's density determines whether or not the liquid it's placed in can offset the pull of gravity on the object and push it up, allowing the object to float instead of sink. Density depends on weight and size, so if two objects are different sizes but weigh the same, the smaller object is the denser one. Ocean liners, freighters, and sloops may be large, but they're all hollow inside, which makes their overall density less than that of water—and that's why they float rather than sink.

◆

SPAM is an acronym for shoulder pork and ham.

TURN TO THE CHASE

We use the phrase "cut to the chase" to cue someone to hurry a story along. And although it sounds like a movie director's request for a quick move to an action scene, it was not first heard on the screen: its first known usage was as a script direction in a 1927 novel, *Hollywood Girl*.

HOLE-Y COW

Bacteria? How can something so bad taste so good? Yet bacteria are essential for making cheese, and different kinds of bacteria give each cheese a specific flavor. *Propionibacter shermani* is just one of three species of bacteria that go into the making of Swiss cheese, but it's the one that makes it holey. As the cheese is being made, the bacteria produce bubbles of carbon dioxide, which leave the distinctive holes—"eyes" is the technical term—that make Swiss so different from all other cheeses.

STOP IT, I LOVE IT!

How is it that being tickled can drive you crazy—and yet when you try to tickle yourself in the very same place, it doesn't work? From birth, stimuli begin to bombard you; one of the first things an infant learns to do is filter them. Consequently, the first signals you ignore are the ones that your own body produces. It's why you don't notice your vocal cords, blinking, the feel of your feet on the sidewalk . . . or self-tickling. The laughter that erupts when someone else is after you is sheer panic.

DID I DO THAT?

When you have a few drinks, your body reacts the same way every time. Once alcohol enters the bloodstream, different parts of the brain are affected, one by one:

Part of Brain Affected	Effect on Behavior
Cerebral cortex	Inhibition of language and information processing
Limbic system	Mood and attitude changes, leading to strong emotion, depression, pursuit of sexual activity
Cerebellum	Changes in coordination and cognition
Hypothalamus and pituitary gland	Increases blood pressure and decreases body temperature
Medulla	Effects on respiration, heart rate, and other vital functions

GLIMPSES OF THE SOUL

The onus of bad luck in breaking a mirror is a comparatively modern version of an ancient belief. Before mirrors, when people checked their appearance in a pool of water, many believed that they were actually seeing a glimpse of their soul. If their reflections were disrupted in any way—a breeze, a stone, a sudden wave—their soul was disturbed as well, and bad luck would befall the viewer.

A DIFFERENT STRIPE

For centuries, stripes have been worn by social outcasts—
serfs, prostitutes, jugglers, clowns, hangmen, Jews, lepers,
cripples, and heretics, to name just a few. Eventually, stripes
adorned the uniforms in most prison systems around the
world.

In the United States, the striped outfits were meant to
symbolize just what they look like: prison bars. During the
Great Depression, many Americans ended up in jail for
crimes that were poverty-related, such as petty theft, va-
grancy, and debt, and prison uniforms changed to jeans and
denim shirts, partly as a way to lessen the humiliation these
first-and-only-time offenders experienced or felt. Today,
many states are returning to the old-fashioned stripes to
make prisoners easy to spot. And for the record, they sell for
about $12 a set and are available in red, green, orange, and
blue stripes on a white ground—although the black-and-
white version is by far the best seller.

THIN STRIPES AND PINSTRIPES

The New York Yankees are famous for their pinstriped home
uniforms, but both stories of how their uniforms came to fea-
ture the stripes are false. Some say they were used to disguise the gigantic girth of the Bambino, Babe Ruth. But the
truth is, the Yankees were already playing in stripes both
before Ruth joined the team and while he was still in shape.
Others say the Yankees thought the moving stripes would
distract the competition during play. But the Bronx Bombers
were just jumping on the fashion bandwagon: the fad for
stripes had started in other clubs years before.

WHO THE HECK IS OLLIE?

However you used to say it as a kid, "Ollie, Ollie, oxen free," "Ollie, Ollie, enfry," or whatever, all agree it was the universal call for every game player still out in the field to come on in. Most likely, kids originally called, "All the outs in free."

NO STRINGS ATTACHED?

Why don't spiders get caught in their own webs? Seems they've got a terrific sense of both design and direction. It helps that the tips of their legs secrete an oily substance to help them slip over the sticky threads they've woven. But the real trick is that not all of the threads in a spiderweb are sticky. The silk for the hub and the spokes radiating out from it are not, but the thread spiders use to make the spiral portion of the web is sticky, to ensnare insects. The spiders know which is which, of course, and manage to sidestep the danger.

FALL INTO . . .

In 1969 a man named Donald Fisher opened a store that sold only records, cassette tapes, and every size of Levi's imaginable—important stuff that parents wouldn't understand because of the generation gap. He named his store . . . The Gap.

◆

Though COLORBLINDNESS is mostly a genetic dysfunction, it can also be caused by nerve or brain damage or by drug use. It occurs in 5–8 percent of men and only 0.5 percent of women.

JUST-WAR THEORY

Why war? Most historians will agree that St. Augustine originated just-war theory, perhaps the most influential perspective on the ethics of war and peace. According to the Hague and Geneva Conventions, just-war theory can be divided into three parts:

1. *Jus ad bellum*, which concerns the justice of resorting to war in the first place:

Just cause
Right intention
Proper authority and public declaration
Last resort
Probability of success
Macro-proportionality—weighing the universal goods expected to result from the war against the universal evils

Just-war theory insists all six criteria must each be fulfilled for a particular declaration of war to be justified.

2. *Jus in bello*, which concerns the justice of conduct within war, after it has begun:

Discrimination—soldiers are only entitled to target those who are "engaged in harm."
Micro-proportionality—soldiers may only use force proportional to the end they seek
No means *mala in se*—soldiers may not use weapons or methods that are "evil in themselves," e.g., mass rape, genocide, ethnic cleansing, or torture

3. *Jus post bellum,* which concerns the justice of peace agreements and the termination phase of war:

Just cause for termination
Right intention
Public declaration and legitimate authority
Discrimination—between, e.g., police, government officials, general population
Proportionality—the terms of peace must be proportional to vindication

(Stanford Encyclopedia of Philosophy)

◆

LIAR, LIAR

A recent study shows that most people lie in everyday conversation, mainly to appear to be more likable and competent. Nearly 60 percent of the people tested in the study lied at least twice during a ten-minute telephone call. Women tend to lie to make the person they're speaking to feel good, while men lie to make themselves look better.

BECAUSE I'M THE AUTHOR

Many science fiction writers use what's called the "tooth fairy rule," which states that a mysterious outside force may be invoked once—but only once—per story to explain away the inexplicable.

◆

The modern NECKTIE is a descendant of the cloths worn by Roman orators around their necks to keep their vocal cords warm. Subsequently they became clothing that proclaimed status, occupation, or identity.

UBER-BRRR?

Though people talk about whether it's "too cold to snow," it's more accurate to ponder whether it's too *dry* to snow. Heavy snowfalls occur when the temperature is right around the freezing point—warmer air holds more moisture than cold air. The conditions for snow include saturated air and an air temperature profile that allows snow to reach the surface. In a city such as Buffalo, New York, its close proximity to Lake Erie results in the perfect moisture-rich conditions to guarantee a large annual snowfall—cold arctic air moving over the warmer surface of the lake picks up moisture and is cooled as it rises, creating clouds and eventually snow.

A STARRY, STARRY POISONED NIGHT

Much has been made of Vincent Van Gogh's mental illness and early death, but it seems his addictions could very well have hastened his demise. Not only was he an alcoholic, but his drinks of choice were paint thinner and the "green fairy," absinthe. It's also possible that Van Gogh was poisoned by digitalis, a common treatment at the time for epilepsy, with which he was afflicted. Many experts believe his digitalis use accounts for his depiction of haloed light sources, as the drug often causes ultrasensitivity to light.

GLASS OR PLASTIC?

Why is it when you go to unload the top rack of the dishwasher, the glass is nice and dry while the plastic containers are still dripping with water? Because glass is a better heat conductor than plastic and therefore dries faster.

WHICH COLOR IS BETTER
FOR CHOCOLATE?

If you thought you were getting cheated out of your favorite color of M&M's in your last bag, you're probably not alone. The numbers of each color are controlled and are a result of heavy consumer testing. Here's the color mix, in percentages:

Flavor	Brown	Yellow	Red	Green	Orange	Blue
Plain	3	14	13	16	20	24
Peanut	12	15	12	15	23	23
Peanut butter	10	20	10	20	20	20
Almond	10	20	10	20	20	20

BUGGY

Life imitates art imitates science? The word *bug* used as a term for a problem in technology (now most often computers) was yet another Edison innovation. He coined the word in 1889 while working on the phonograph; it was an expression he evidently used when he ran into difficulty, implying that there was an imaginary bug inside, wreaking havoc. Over half a century later in 1947, the bug joke was picked up by computer geeks when a moth flew into the Mark II computer at Harvard University and actually stopped up the works. The bug was captured, taped down, and logged in. The entry? "First actual case of bug being found."

◆

A PRINCIPALITY is a sovereign territory that is ruled by a prince or princess.

EDWARD BARLEYCORN

It was no mathematician but King Edward I of England who standardized measurements back in 1305. He dictated that an inch would be defined as the length of "three barleycorns, round and dry." His purpose was to set a standard of accuracy in certain trades; British cobblers were among the first to adopt the idea.

TRADE AGREEMENT

Back in the day, a betrothal was much more of a family affair. The bride's dowry, set by her parents, was something substantial, equal to the bride's perceived worth and meant to bring value to the marriage. The groom did his part, too, by paying a brideprice to her family, which helped pay for the wedding costs, and by promising to support her faithfully.

FINE FRIGID FRIENDS?

Why is it we humans need cashmere and snowsuits to keep warm, while birds fly about year-round only in feather suits? Frankly, our heating systems aren't as good.

In human bodies, the further hot blood is pumped from the heart, the more it cools. Birds' circulatory systems, on the other hand, have a different kind of network, called a *rete mirabile*, or "wondrous network." A bird's arteries lie extremely close to the veins, so close that their proximity causes heat to be evenly transferred from the warmer artery to the cooler vein. That's why, for birds, feathers are enough, and they're virtually always warm all over.

THE BAD-TEMPERED LILY

The onion is a member of the lily family. Such a nice family . . . and yet the onion has a reputation as a tearjerker. When you slice an onion, you release sulfur compounds that evaporate and become a volatile gas, and that gas irritates eyes. Slicing the onion under running water helps—many of the sulfur compounds will dissolve in water. Cutting out the root first works, too, because that's where the compounds originate.

ANIMAL LOGIC

"Hair of the dog" is only part of the longer, original expression, "the hair of the dog that bit you." People used to believe that the antidote for a dog bite should include some of the guilty dog's hair. Same for a hangover: a little more of the same should set everything straight.

NUMBER, PLEASE
Why does every movie character live in the same neighborhood?

Surely you've noticed: Every single solitary time a phone number is given on TV or in the movies, it's strangely familiar. First, the appropriate area code—but after that? The exchange always seems to be "555," or, in older cases, "Klondike 5." It's because 555 is reserved for information nationwide in the United States. So any, er, fan who tries to call the number the pretty girl just gave the handsome detective is guaranteed to be out of luck.

FABULISTS

Aesop's fables, Mother Goose, nursery rhymes—speculations
on their origins are numerous. Historians are split as to
whether Aesop was born a slave or even existed at all.
Mother Goose may be the pseudonym of Queen Bertha of
France. But by the seventeenth century, nursery rhymes
were imbedded in culture, with roots in tales centuries old.
Based in oral tradition, they disappear and resurface, sometimes slightly changed. Many historians believe the versions
of nursery rhymes we know today concern themselves with
British history and personalities. Some theories:

A FROG HE WOULD A-WOOING GO . . .
So there's an end of one, two, and three, the Rat,
the Mouse, and little Froggy.

Concerns a French suitor of Queen Elizabeth I, the Duke of
Anjou, who was not successful in his pursuit.

BAA, BAA, BLACK SHEEP . . .
One for the master,
One for the dame,
And one for the little boy
Who lives down the lane.

Having to divide up the bags is said to be about the export
tax on wool in 1275.

GEORGIE, GEORGIE, PUDDING AND PIE . . .
Kissed the girls and made them cry.
When the boys came out to play,
Georgie Porgie ran away.

King George IV apparently enjoyed women and wealth but

was fearful of political reform. Other guesses as to the secret identity of "Georgie" have been King George I, the Duke of Buckingham (George Villiers), and King Charles II.

HICKORY, DICKORY, DOCK . . .
The mouse ran up the clock
The clock struck one
The mouse ran down.

Said to be about Richard Cromwell, who could neither preserve the republic put in place by his father, Oliver Cromwell, nor prevent the restoration of the monarchy.

HUMPTY DUMPTY SAT ON A WALL . . .
Humpty Dumpty had a great fall.
All the king's horses and all the king's men
Couldn't put Humpty together again.

Though some believe the original Humpty to be King Richard III, it most likely refers to King John's loss of power to the barons.

JACK AND JILL WENT UP THE HILL . . .
To fetch a pail of water.
Jack fell down and broke his crown,
And Jill came tumbling after.

A ditty about the failure of a plan to marry Queen Mary I to the King of France.

JACK SPRATT COULD EAT NO FAT . . .
His wife could eat no lean.
And so between the two of them,
They licked the platter clean.

This is allegedly about King Charles I and his wife, Queen Henrietta, who were quite opposite in their personalities.

LITTLE BOY BLUE, COME BLOW YOUR HORN . . .
The sheep's in the meadow,
The cow's in the corn.
But where is the boy who looks after the sheep?
He's under the haystack,
Fast asleep.
Little Boy Blue is Cardinal Wolsey, who was "found asleep"
by King Henry VIII and lost his power when he could not
win the King a divorce. (Wolsey was a butcher's son, who
undoubtedly looked after his father's livestock.)

LITTLE JACK HORNER SAT IN A CORNER . . .
Eating a Christmas pie:
He put in his thumb and pulled out a plum,
And said, "What a good boy am I!"
A story about the English Reformation, when Henry VIII
became Protestant and seized all Roman Catholic Church
properties, especially the monasteries.

LITTLE MISS MUFFET SAT ON A TUFFET . . .
Eating her curds and whey.
Along came a spider,
Who sat down beside her,
And frightened Miss Muffet away.
Mary, Queen of Scots, is Miss Muffet, and a Catholic who
displeased the Presbyterian preacher John Knox, who stars as
the frightening arachnid.

OLD MOTHER HUBBARD WENT TO THE CUPBOARD . . .
To give her poor dog a bone.
But when she got there, her cupboard was bare,
And so the poor dog had none.

This describes Cardinal Wolsey's efforts to compensate himself for loss of the king's favor by securing various offices and titles.

THREE BLIND MICE, SEE HOW THEY RUN . . .
They all ran after the farmer's wife,
Who cut off their tails with a carving knife.
Did you ever see such a sight in your life,
As three blind mice?

The mice most likely represented Lattimer, Ridley, and Cranmer, Protestant clergymen who died at the stake. The farmer's wife was Queen Mary I.

LIGHTNING GLASS

Lightning strikes somewhere on earth approximately one hundred times per second. The strikes occasionally result in fulgurites, or "lightning glass"—hollow, carrot-shaped tubes formed when a lightning bolt courses through sand at 2,950 degrees Fahrenheit, instantly superheating the sand and melting and fusing its grains. Sand, of course, is commonly used in the manufacture of commercial glass, along with soda ash, limestone, and borax. The largest fulgurite on record was found in Florida and was nearly seventeen feet long.

CHEERS, INDEED!

Ancient Greeks would toast to good health to let guests know that their drinks had not been spiked with poison. A toast requires the host to take the first sip.

THE TWELVE DAYS OF CATECHISM

As Christmas approaches, "The Twelve Days of Christmas" becomes the Yuletide season's "99 Bottles of Beer on the Wall." Its monotony and repetition originally had a purpose, though: it was written as a catechism song. Between the years 1558 and 1829, English Catholics were not permitted to practice their faith, and the song was composed to mask lessons. "My true love" was God himself, and the partridge stood for Jesus Christ. Herewith the rest of the code:

Two turtledoves	The Old and New Testaments
Three French hens	Faith, hope, and charity
Four calling birds	The four Gospels
Five golden rings	The first five books of the Old Testament, which give the history of humankind's fall from grace
Six geese a-laying	The six days of creation
Seven swans a-swimming	The seven gifts of the Holy Spirit
Eight maids a-milking	The eight Beatitudes
Nine ladies dancing	Nine choirs of angels
Ten lords a-leaping	The Ten Commandments
Eleven pipers piping	The eleven faithful Apostles
Twelve drummers drumming	The twelve points of belief in the Apostles' Creed

◆

HERRING PARTS are used in ceramic glazes, nail polish, lipsticks, and even some automobile paint to give them shine. The fish scales are transformed into "pearl essence" to brighten commercial products.

DEAD GRANDMOTHER REDUX

A major job search Web site reports that the three top reasons for calling in sick when you're not sick are:

Personal business and errands
Catching up on sleep
Relaxing

Here are some other reasons—clearly not entirely true—in case you want to be more creative:

Sprayed by a skunk
Tripped over dog and knocked unconscious
Bus broke down and was held up by robbers
Arrested as a result of mistaken identity
Forgot to come back to work after lunch
Couldn't find shoes
Hurt during bowling
Spit on by a venomous snake
Being pursued by a hit man
Scalp burned by curlers
Brain went to sleep
Cat unplugged alarm clock
Had to attend husband's grand jury trial
Forgot what day of the week it was
Got slipped drugs in a drink
Tree fell on car
Pet monkey died

◆

Legend has it that ST. FABIAN was elected pope in 236 because a dove landed on his head, and the clergy took it as an anointment from above.

PREMATURELY, OF COURSE

Whether we embrace it, color it, or blame it on our children, the majority of us can expect our hair to go gray with age. Recent studies have indicated that as we grow older, melanocytes—pigment-producing cells—play a part in not only skin color but hair color as well. The pigment is located in the hair follicle, and when with time these melanocytes become depleted, there goes the golden pate of your youth. (Take heart: scientists in Japan are working with a type of pepper that may reinvigorate the melanocytes.)

FLIGHT SCHOOL

Scientists have long theorized that birds fly in a V formation to gain lift from the bird in front of them—vortices form as a result of the first bird's flight, and the following bird, if in the right position, flies in an area of greatly reduced air resist-ance. Recent discoveries show other benefits of decreased drag: the heart rates of some birds were lower while in formation, allowing then to glide more often and conserve energy. It is believed that a flock of geese can fly 70 percent further while in formation, with birds taking turns as lead flier. The V formation also offers each bird an unobstructed view, so flock members can avoid collisions and communi-cate while in flight.

◆

BENJAMIN FRANKLIN never patented a single one of his inventions. He insisted that he was wealthy enough and that his ideas were for the benefit of the American people, not for his own profit.

FORTY WINKS

Experts say that while a full night's sleep is necessary to restore and perform many vital body functions, a short sleep may boost learning and memory. A 60-to-90-minute nap can be as beneficial to some as a full night's sleep, as long as the napper experiences both slow-wave sleep and rapid eye movement (REM), which are stages of deep sleep. Bosses are also finding that sleep deprivation is all too common among employees and is costing them plenty. Some sleep deprivation consequences in the workplace are:

- Increased errors and accidents
- Increased absenteeism
- Increased drug use
- Increased turnover
- Higher group insurance premiums
- Decreased productivity

A LONG WINTER'S NAP

Animals hibernate for the simplest of reasons: It is their only alternative to starvation. Once cold sets in and food and water become unavailable, these animals find a safe place to sleep, and slow their heartbeat dramatically and lower their body temperature, sometimes to nearly freezing, both of which diminish their need for food.

◆

BLISTERS appear on a patch of skin where damage has occurred—whether from a burn, a pinch, or simply friction. It protects the flesh from further irritation, allowing it a chance to heal.

SINCERE BUT FLOWERY

Since Victorian times, giving different types of flowers as a gift signified different feelings or purposes.

Amaryllis: splendid beauty, pride
Ambrosia: mutual love
Baby's breath: fruitful marriage
Bluebell: constancy
Calla lily: magnificent beauty
Camellia: gratitude
Carnation: strong love, beauty
Chrysanthemum (red): love
Chrysanthemum (white): truth
Cornflower: delicacy
Cyclamen: modesty and shyness
Daffodil: high regard
Daisy: innocence
Dogwood: love's durability
Fern: fascination and beauty
Flowering almond: hope
Forget-me-not: remembrance
Forsythia: anticipation
Geranium: comfort
Heliotrope: devotion, faithfulness
Hibiscus: delicate beauty
Honeysuckle: generosity
Hyacinth (white): loveliness
Hydrangea: boastfulness
Iris: faith, wisdom
Ivy: eternal fidelity
Japonica: loveliness
Jasmine: joy and amiability
Lilac: first love

Lily (white): purity, happiness
Magnolia: love of nature, nobility, dignity
Maidenhair: discretion
Mimosa: sensitivity
Orange blossom: purity, fertility
Orchid: love, beauty
Pansy: think of me
Peach blossom: captivity
Periwinkle: pleasing memories
Rose (red): love
Rose (yellow): friendship
Rose (coral): desire
Rose (peach): modesty
Rose (dark pink): thankfulness
Rose (pale pink): grace
Rose (orange): fascination
Rose (white): innocence
Rosemary: remembrance, loyalty
Sage: wisdom
Snowdrop: hope
Stephanotis: happiness in marriage
Stock: lasting beauty
Sunflower: adoration
Sweet pea: lasting pleasure
Sweet William: sensitivity
Tulip: true love
Verbena (pink): family unity
Veronica: fidelity
Violet: purity, modesty, fidelity
Wheat: prosperity, friendliness

◆

The SWASTIKA was chosen for use by the Nazis because
it is an ancient symbol of prosperity and good fortune.

THE ORIGINAL HOME SHOPPING NETWORK

Much of Sears Roebuck and Company's success came from its early dependency on mail order. Shortly after Richard Sears began to sell watches to railroad station agents like himself in 1886, he wrote and printed a mailer to sell watches and jewelry by mail under the name R. W. Sears Watch Co. This was 1888, and both the westward railroad expansion and the postal system were working in Sears's favor. Not only were the catalogs permitted to be mailed as aids in the dissemination of knowledge (at one cent per pound), but the advent of rural free delivery in 1896 made distribution of the catalog economical. Farmers and others who lived outside of towns and cities began to rely on the Sears catalog, "the Cheapest Supply House on Earth." The catalog expanded from watches and jewelry, adding sewing machines, sporting goods, musical instruments, saddles, firearms, buggies, bicycles, baby carriages, clothing, and eyeglasses. Nearly every word was written by Sears himself, using familiar stories and personal experiences to sell his wares, much the same way many of today's most successful mail order catalogs and Internet companies do.

FORE . . . AND A QUARTER

The universal diameter for a golf cup is 4¼ inches. It started when a particular hole at St. Andrews in Scotland continually filled with sand after a period of rain. Two golfers found a drainpipe—it happened to be 4¼ inches—and absconded with a piece to temporarily stem the tide of wet sand. It was the first "cup" installed on the course, and became the standard at St. Andrews and subsequently the world.

PUT A HOLE IN ONE

There are two schools of thought on why the doughnut has a hole—and both have the ring of truth. The first is based in logic: The fried cakes bakers made would often be too doughy in the middle if cooked until the outer part was done, but too crisp around the edges if left to fry a little longer. A hole was the perfect solution for even cooking.

Captain Hanson Gregory is at the center of the second theory. While at the helm of his ship one stormy night, he found it impossible to get a good grip on the helm while eating his fried cake. He impaled the pastry on one of the wheel's spokes, forming a temporary rest area for the cake and a long-term culinary delight for posterity.

NOW AND LATER

It sounds like something from outer space: microencapsulation. But actually it's the secret behind scratch 'n' sniff. The essence of a fragrance is distilled into a perfume so that millions of tiny bubbles are suspended in a liquid; this is then incorporated into a plastic that can be used and printed like ink. After the plastic dries, the trapped fragrance is released from a few bubbles each time the area is activated. That's why a scratch 'n' sniff item can last for years—this microencapsulation process holds each drop of fragrance better than if it were in a stoppered bottle.

◆

MAYDAY, the international radio distress call, has nothing to do with traditional spring celebrations—the French term *m'aider*, or "help me," has merely become anglicized.

NEW YEAR—IT'S WHAT YOU EAT

It's universal to wish others happiness and good luck at the new year. Some countries believe eating special food will help that good fortune along:

Belarus: Each piece of meat eaten during New Year's Eve dinner brings your happiness.

Germany: Eating carp is thought to be such good luck that people place some of the fish's scales in their wallets for financial good fortune.

Holland: For good luck in the new year the Dutch eat *olie bollen*, puffy doughnuts filled with diced apples, raisins, and currants.

Hungary: Eat something sweet for the first bite in the New Year so that the whole year is sweet. No chicken or fish for New Year's Day lunch and dinner: Fish swim away with your luck, chickens scratch it away. Lentils and pork will bring wealth, health, and luck.

Ireland: This one's not for consumption: Bang on the door and walls with Christmas bread to chase the bad luck out and bring good spirits to the household, along with the promise of enough food for the new year.

Italy: Drinking beer after midnight brings good luck. For New Year's Day supper, have thirteen courses for good fortune. Caviar will bring you riches all the year. Lentils and *zampone* (a stuffed pig's trotter) bring luck. Chickpeas bring health and fortune. And *chiacchiere*, honey-drenched balls of dough, ensure a sweet year. (Slip some of those lentils in your purse for luck, too.)

Korea: *Ttokguk,* or rice cake soup, is eaten as part of sunrise celebrations. Koreans believe that each bowl eaten adds a year to your life.

Mexico, Spain, and Cuba: These countries enjoy a custom of eating twelve grapes at the stroke of midnight while making twelve wishes, each grape signifying one month of the upcoming year. If the grape for the respective month is sweet, expect a good month; if it's sour, the month will be a bad one.

Philippines: Food on the table at midnight encourages an abundance of food throughout the year.

Poland: Folklore suggests that eating herring at the stroke of midnight will bring luck for the next year.

Scotland: The first one who draws and drinks water from a well will be lucky, usually in love: "The flower o' the well to our howse gaes / And the bonniest lad'll be mine."

Slovakia: Cut an apple, and if the seeds are healthy, you will be, too. Mothers cross their children with honey on their foreheads for a sweet life.

Southern United States: Black-eyed peas are eaten for luck, with corn bread, cabbage, collard greens, or kale for wealth.

Worldwide: In many places, eating ring-shaped food (doughnuts especially) symbolizes coming full circle, and good luck will follow. Cabbage is also considered a sign of prosperity.

FLAG WAVING

When you see flag decals on a bus, plane, or taxi, the flag's field of stars should be on the left side when placed on the left side of the vehicle. But on the right side of the vehicle, the decal should be placed with the stars facing right so that the flag will appear as if the vehicle's forward motion is causing the flag to blow in the wind.

WHAT A DUMB HAT

John Duns Scotus, an influential thirteenth-century philosopher, founded a school of scholasticism known as Scotism. Over time, Scotism fell out of fashion, and his followers, thought of as tedious hairsplitters, became known as "Dunses." Scotus believed that conical hats were an aid to brainpower (look at wizards, for example), and insisted that they funnel knowledge to the wearer. Eventually Scotus's "Duns caps"—later called dunce caps—were objects of ridicule and by the nineteenth century students were forced to wear them as a symbol of shame.

MURDER MOST FRIENDLY

What's a little homicide between pals—at least in the United States, Canada, or Greece? In these countries, friends or acquaintances account for almost half of all killings. In the majority of cases, there's a single victim and a single offender; most often both are male. The scene of the crime is frequently a residence, with both victim and offender having been drinking.

AM I BORING YOU?

You may not be tired, and it's been proven that it has nothing to do with lack of oxygen. Yawning is contagious, and just thinking about it right now may cause you to open wide.

Sometimes yawning is a response to a visual stimulus. Scientists point to mirror neurons, which cause people to react with the same behavior they sense in someone else. Up to 60 percent of people who watch a video or hear others talk about yawning are apt to follow suit. And others believe that it's an evolutionary remnant that communicates a need for rest or a desire to be alone (which explains our feeling that we're boring someone when they yawn).

Other interesting things about yawning:

- After the age of five, children begin to yawn contagiously.
- Schizophrenics rarely yawn.
- Yawning often precedes a major activity change—thus an athlete may yawn while in the starting blocks, a soprano before the curtain goes up.

SMALL STUFF

What of the word *trivia* itself? In medieval times, education was divided into seven sections. The sciences were arithmetic, geometry, astronomy, and music; the liberal studies were grammar, rhetoric, and logic. The former list of studies—the quadrivium, which is from the Latin for "four ways"—was thought to consist of the more important subjects. The other, more general group of three was known as the trivium, and thus anything learned on these subjects was, well, trivial.

SOME WHO HAVE ASKED WHY

"There is occasions and causes why and
wherefore in all things."
—WILLIAM SHAKESPEARE, HENRY V

"Why don't you speak for yourself, John?"
—HENRY WADSWORTH LONGFELLOW,
"THE COURTSHIP OF MILES STANDISH"

"Every why hath a wherefore."
—WILLIAM SHAKESPEARE, THE COMEDY OF ERRORS

"You see things; and you say, 'Why?' But I dream things
that never were; and I say 'Why not?'"
—GEORGE BERNARD SHAW, BACK TO METHUSELAH
(quoted by and often misattributed to
Robert F. Kennedy)

"Love's stricken 'why'
Is all that love can speak—
Built of but just a syllable
The hugest hearts that break."
—EMILY DICKINSON, "NO. 1368"

"My advice to you is not to inquire why or
whither, but just enjoy your ice cream while it's on
your plate—that's my philosophy."
—THORNTON WILDER, THE SKIN OF OUR TEETH

"Saul. Saul, why persecutest thou me?"
—ACTS OF THE APOSTLES 9:4

YOU WORM!

First of all, it's not tequila, it's mescal. That's where you'll find the worm at the bottom of the bottle. There's even some logic for it being there: It's the agave worm (actually a butterfly larva), found on the plant mescal is made from. Many believe that the worm (which was very nearly nixed recently by Mexican officials as too low-class) is an essential component to the alcohol's *je ne sais quoi*. Not only does it add to mescal's flavor and color, they insist, but the worm brings good luck. And some even go so far as to say it's an aphrodisiac.

HIGHWAYS OR SKYWAYS?

General—and subsequently President—Dwight D. Eisenhower was extremely impressed during his World War II stay in Germany with the Germans' well-designed autobahn system. It led him to a crack world leader–cum–military genius idea of his own. All the interstate highways that were planned in the United States during the Eisenhower administration required that one mile in every five be straight. These straight sections would be usable as airstrips in times of war or other emergencies.

◆

The term JAILBIRD was coined in England centuries ago, when criminals were placed in cages, which were then hung three feet off the ground.

The main reason people want to remove their TATTOOS is that they have fallen out of love with the person they've memorialized on their body in ink.

FIELDS OF GLORY

The miles of breathtaking tulip fields in Holland are a beautiful sight to see. But why the Netherlands . . . and why tulips?

The popular perennial is actually indigenous to central Asia; in fact, the Turks of the Ottoman Empire were the botanists who really took to the tulip and began to cultivate it with ardor as early as 1000 C.E. The tulips that Europeans eventually imported now grow in parts of Russia, around the Black Sea, and the Crimea.

In the 1500s, with world exploration on the rise, Europeans became obsessed with the importation of beautiful flowers. Botanical drawings became popular to hang in one's parlor, tulip drawings chief among them. This fueled what was becoming "Tulip Mania," though this frenzy was largely driven by a botanist named Carolus Clusius, who in 1593 was appointed the head botanist, or *Hortulanus*, at the University of Leiden's Hortus, the first botanical garden in Western Europe. Clusius had befriended a man named de Busbecq, an ambassador to Constantinople, who had given him some tulip bulbs—long thought to be a sign of wealth and power in the Ottoman Empire—which he brought back to Holland. Though Clusius's interest in the tulips was scientific, the combination of the drawings, the plants' rarity, and their foreign popularity proved too much for the Dutch, and some of Clusius's bulbs were stolen. Now Tulip Mania was in full swing.

Prices skyrocketed, and tulip buying and trading became heavy. Hybrids became coveted, with prices as high as $1,500 per bulb for a flower we can purchase today for about fifty cents; the highest recorded trade for a single bloom was

$2,250 plus a horse and carriage. Prices eventually settled down, and the Dutch have made tulip exporting one of the most successful businesses in the world. About 7 million of the 9 million tulips grown there are sold in other countries, at a value of $750 million. And that still leaves enough for locals and tourists to enjoy.

A romantic tulip aside: While the rose is universally thought of as the most romantic of flowers, there is a Turkish fable about Prince Farhad and his lady love, Shirin. Inconsolable upon hearing that she had been killed, the prince rode his horse off a cliff to his own death. It is said that for every drop of blood he shed, a red tulip sprang up in her memory, making the tulip the Turkish symbol of perfect love, and Turkey's national flower.

DIAL-A-RIDDLE

Why—and when—did zero become the number after nine? Look around: cell phones and remote controls are just a couple of places numbers are set up like this, though calculators still have the zero preceding the number one.

It's a throwback to the old rotary phones, when the telephone signal was a series of pulses, and zero, needing to have ten pulses, logically appeared on the dial after the nine. When touch-tone phones came on the market and the numbers started to appear in a grid, the zero followed the nine, because that's what people expected.

◆

The human STOMACH needs to produce a new layer of mucus every two weeks, or digestive acids will cause it to digest itself.

FEET ON THE GROUND

Men atop their mounts have long been a paean to famous or fallen leaders, and over the centuries the belief has grown that the number of horse's hooves touching the ground on a statue has to do with the fate of the rider. This is the supposed relationship of the rider's posture and the way he died:

> If the horse has both front legs in the air, the rider died in battle.

> If the horse has only one front leg in the air, the rider died as the result of wounds suffered while in battle.

> If the horse has all four feet on the ground, the rider died of natural causes.

Recent research by buffs suggests the legend may be untrue. Most of the statues at Gettysburg do comply with the rules, save one, however, so some say this is where the notion began. The exception: The horse of General John F. Reynolds, who was killed at Gettysburg, has one foreleg and one hind leg raised, instead of both forelegs.

COPYCAT

When the Haloid Company set out to brand its electrophotography machine, they hired a scholar of classical languages to come up with a name. He suggested the process be called xerography, from the Greek words for "dry" and "writing." The copier itself he named the Xerox machine.

SEEING EYES

One of the many dark surprises of growing older is that our vision begins to fail. By your forties, you may find the menu in a candlelit restaurant hard to read, instructions on a pill bottle impossible to read. You've got presbyopia, and you can't put it off anymore: You need reading glasses or bifocals. If glasses on a beaded chain around your neck don't appeal, what do you do? Now there are bifocal contact lenses.

Like bifocal glasses, there are two prescriptions per lens—one to see things up close, and one for distance. But since contact lenses float in your eye and don't stay perched on your nose where you can control exactly where to look, how do they know? How *do* they work?

Here are the three types currently available, and how they're made:

Aspheric: Prescriptions for both near and distance vision are close to the middle of the lens, though the near prescription is at the center.

Concentric: The near prescription is in the middle of the lens, while the prescription for distance is around the outside.

Translating: The near prescription is on the bottom, and the distance prescription is on the top. The bottom part of the contact is flat, as if the bottom of a circle were cut off, so that it doesn't rotate when you blink.

Some doctors may instead prescribe two completely different lenses—one eye for distance, the other for close work: a dizzying effect for a bit, but once their eyes adjust, many people swear by this method.

LAUGH, LAUGH, LAUGH

The human being is the only species capable of laughter as we know—and hear—it. On average, we experience it seventeen times a day. And it not only feels good—it really *is* good for you, healthwise:

- It reduces our stress levels by reducing the level of stress hormones
- It helps us cope with serious illnesses
- It promotes healing by lowering the blood pressure
- It increases vascular blood flow
- It increases oxygenation of the blood

And though we do talk of "breaking" or "bursting" into laughter, it is a quite orderly communicative response. It may feel spontaneous, but in fact it occurs during pauses in conversation or at the end of stories, after the punch line. This is why scientists call it the "punctuation effect."

Laughter is triggered not only by humor, but by sociological or psychological situations: when people are comfortable with each other, shared relief, the passing of danger, social situations that need easing. The brain responds simultaneously with both sound and movement: not only are our facial muscles involved, but there are involuntary movements in the muscles of the arms, legs, and trunk as well.

◆

The RABBIT'S FOOT is considered good luck because the rabbit, with its ability to reproduce at astonishing speed, was seen as a symbol of fertility.

MONEY FROM THE SEA

The Narragansett Indians of New England were the first to use wampum, cylindrical beads to measure value. It preceded the use of currency in the United States by several hundred years but was used most often not as money, but as trade; when woven into intricate belts and other jewelry, it was a means of solemnizing agreements.

Wampum is actually a mispronunciation of the Narragansett word for the inner part of the whelk shell, *wompam*. The purple beads were valued at five times more than the white ones. The beads were often strung and measured on a six-foot string, which they dubbed a "fathom," echoing the sea term. Eventually, wampum use became more widespread, and it was used for a wider variety of transactions. Historians note that wampum was used for ransom for captives, compensation for crimes, presents between friends, prizes for victory in games or sport, paying fines, incentives to maintain peace or to wage war, payments for services of shamanism, marriage proposals, and, possibly, bribes and rewards for murder. Perhaps the most unusual payment? One could pay for an education at Harvard with wampum beads.

ON THE CLOCK

Clocks run clockwise most likely because they were made to run the same way a sundial did. Both the sundial and the clock were invented in the Northern Hemisphere, and the east-to-west direction of the sun during the day causes the shade on a sundial to run clockwise—or sundialwise. All would be different if the sundial had been invented in the southern hemisphere.

THE WHY OF WHO

An eponym is the name of a person for whom something is supposedly named. But why do they come into use? A few reasons and examples:

- By association with a person (derrick)
- In honor of (einsteinium)
- Infamy (bowdlerize)
- Interjections (Geronimo!)
- Invention (shrapnel)
- Metonymy ("Dad burned the steaks on the Weber")
- Possessives and Compound Nouns (Planck's constant, Doppler effect)
- "Pulled a _____." (Winona)
- Self-promotion (daguerreotype)
- Simple metaphor (quisling)
- With Suffixes
  - -esque (Kafkaesque)
  - -ia (dahlia)
  - -ian/-ean (Orwellian)
  - -ism (spoonerism)
  - -ite (rammelsburgite)
  - -ium (curium)
  - -ize (grangerize)
  - -mander (gerrymander)
  - -phone (sousaphone)
  - -type (daguerreotype)
- Trademark (Frisbee)
- "Verbing" (boycott, lynch)

WHAT PRICE, BEAUTY?
From the "Don't Try This at Home" Files

In what was thought of as a great improvement, the Romans changed the basic toothpaste formula concocted by the Egyptians in the fourth century. Various mixtures were used early on: One was salt, pepper, mint leaves, and irises; a later concoction was crushed pumice stone and wine vinegar. The Romans replaced the vinegar with human urine, which contains ammonia, a whitening agent. In the eighteenth century, straight ammonia took its place.

SMELLY LOGIC

Perhaps it's not the very best food for your social life*, but there are plenty of healthy reasons to keep garlic in one's diet. In fact, for more than five thousand years, the good clove has been said to heal everything from snakebites to the plague. Some of today's more popular uses:

- It lowers the risk of stomach cancer
- Studies show it may impede other cancers
- It helps hypertension
- It may help prevent heart disease
- It can lower blood cholesterol
- It can even be used as an antiseptic, killing fungus and some types of bacteria
- It clears acne in its raw form
- It's a natural mosquito repellent
- It prevents cold and flu

*You can always try the less-pungent pill form.

THE MARCH (AND MAY AND JULY) OF TIME

The months of the year—and for that matter, the entire year itself—went through several permutations before the advent of the Gregorian calendar, which is the one in use by most of the world today. In the Roman calendar, which is thought to have been constructed by Romulus, Rome's founder, there were only ten months (which is why, for example, September, the ninth month, is named with the Latin root for the word seven). The year was then only 304 days long; harsh winter times without any agricultural activity remained unnamed; and the new moon in March started another year, in line with the lunar cycle. With the reign of Rome's second king, Numa Pompilius (c. 700 C.E.), what are now the first two months of the year were added.

Julius Caesar abolished the lunar year and implemented a calendar ruled by the sun. The new length of the Julian calendar year was 365 days, with an extra day every four years. Now we had twelve months and a leap year.

The Gregorian calendar was devised by Neapolitan Aloysius Lilius, and adopted in 1582 by Pope Gregory XIII, basically to correct the errors of the Julian calendar; now the tropical year would be 365 97/400 days.

So the months of the year are, not surprisingly, an array of words composed of Latin roots, Roman gods, and unanswered questions:

January: After Janus, the Roman god of beginnings, doors, sunrise, and sunset. He had one face that looked forward and one that looked back.

February: Romans celebrated *februa* the festival of forgiveness (from the Latin "to purify").

March: The first month of the old Roman year, it is named after Mars, the god of war.

April: Possibly from *aperire*, "to open," signaling the signs of spring; or perhaps from Aphrodite, original Greek name of Venus.

May: Probably from a Roman goddess: either from Maiesta, the Roman goddess of honor, or Maia, mother of Mercury.

June: Named to honor Juno, the chief Roman goddess.

July: This was the month Julius Caesar was born, and named for him in 44 B.C.E., the year of his assassination.

August: Formerly called Sextilis (the sixth month in the Roman calendar), it was renamed in 8 B.C.E. to honor Augustus Caesar.

September: *Septem*, Latin for seven in the Roman calendar.

October: The eighth month (*octo* in Latin) in the Roman calendar.

November: The ninth Roman month, from *novem*.

December: *Decem*, for the Roman tenth month.

The word BALLOT comes from *balotta*, the Italian word for "ball" or "small pebble," the latter of which was used in ancient times to cast a vote.

SEE THROUGH

The reason we can see through glass is the same reason we can see through water: they're both liquids. As opposed to most liquids, which basically remain the same color, opaqueness, and viscosity, glass becomes stiffer as it cools. At room temperature, its rate of flow is so slow that it would virtually never lose its shape. Formally the scientific term used for glass was "supercooled liquid;" this implies that in the process of being made, the glass has been rapidly chilled past its normal freezing point, and though for all intents and purposes looks and acts like a solid, its loosely spaced molecular structure allows for light to pass through, and thus ensures its clarity. More recently, the term "amorphous solid" is more often applied; this refers to an apparently solid substance that lacks crystalline structure, and instead has the random organization of liquids.

Need it be said? In the case of glass, seeing is *not* believing.

SEASON FOR SNEEZIN'

Sneezing, of course, expels whatever is bothering you and your nose, whether it's dust, pepper, or even cold air. But it's not just the nose that gets the message. Lots of different muscles have to react all at once in order for the process to take place. Abdominal muscles, the diaphragm, vocal chords, and even eyelid muscles work all at once. And then there are photic sneezers, who *ahchoo* when they are exposed to bright light; one in three people do it, and there's no way to cure yourself of it. It's inherited.

CHOOSING POLITICAL SIDES

Have you ever noticed how people tend to take the same seat, if it's available, in a recurring situation? At the dinner table, in a classroom, at a meeting, everyone tends to gravitate to the same chair, time after time. It's thought that this is how the terms Left and Right began for political liberals and conservatives.

When the French legislature met for the first time after the French Revolution, in October 1791, all 745 members arrived and looked to sit with their like-minded friends. It so happened that the radicals sat on the left side of the room, with the more traditional-minded people choosing seats to the right of the aisle. A custom—and a new way of defining politics—had begun.

LIFE BLOOD

Top 10 reasons people give the Red Cross for not giving blood:

1. I don't like needles / I am afraid to give blood.
2. I'm too busy.
3. No one ever asked me—I didn't realize my blood was needed.
4. I already gave this year.
5. I'm afraid I'll get AIDS.
6. My blood isn't the right type.
7. I don't have any blood to spare.
8. I don't want to feel weak afterward.
9. They won't want my blood (I am too old / I've had an illness).
10. I have a rare blood type, so I'll wait until there is a special need.

WHY CAN'T I GO?

Why is a movie unsuitable for kids (or for your very own precious ears and eyes)? Is it raunchy, trash-talking, or pornographic? Actually, the movie rating system—a voluntary system sponsored by the Motion Picture Association of America and the National Association of Theatre Owners—was designed to guide people with just a little bit of generalized advance warning on what types of things might take place when the lights go down.

General Audience—All ages are admitted. This film contains nothing most parents will consider offensive for even their youngest children to see or hear. Nudity, sex scenes, and scenes of drug use are absent; violence is minimal; snippets of dialogue may go beyond polite conversation but do not go beyond common everyday expressions.

Parental Guidance Suggested—Some material may not be suitable for children. Explicit sex scenes and scenes of drug use are absent; nudity, if present, is seen only briefly, horror and violence do not exceed moderate levels.

Parents Strongly Cautioned—Some material may be inappropriate for children under 13. Rough or persistent violence is absent; sexually-oriented nudity is generally absent; some scenes of drug use may be seen; one use of the harsher sexually derived words may be heard.

Restricted: Under 17—Requires an accompanying parent or adult guardian. An R may be assigned due to, among other things, a film's use of language, theme, violence, sex, or its portrayal of drug use.

No One 17 and Under Admitted—The rating board believes that most American parents would feel that the film is patently adult. May contain explicit sex scenes, an accumulation of sexually oriented language, or scenes of excessive violence. Does not, however, signify that the rated film is obscene or pornographic.

◆

THE DIRT

Pica is an eating disorder quite unlike the types one reads about in magazines. It is an addictive craving for non-food substances such as dirt, clay, chalk, even ice chips. It is seen mostly in pregnant women, children, or third world countries where there may be a mineral-deficient diet. The name *pica* comes from the Latin word for magpie, a kind of bird known for its reputation to eat almost everything. Geophagy—eating dirt or clay—is a common form of pica; particular types of chalky dirt are sold in stores in parts of the southern United States. Native Americans concoct a form of acorn bread today in which clay is an important ingredient.

EYES WIDE SHUT

It sounds like something we only read about, on top of just sounding plain suspicious, but hysterical blindness is real. It's called conversion disorder, and is a psychiatric condition in which emotional distress expresses itself through physical symptoms. Inability to speak and paralysis are other forms of the disease. The symptom, though not usually life-threatening in itself, usually—and often spontaneously—disappears in the space of a few days or weeks.

COMATOSE

A coma is an extended period of unconsciousness from which a person may or may not eventually recover; while in a deep coma, one cannot be aroused with even the most painful stimuli. One can fall into a coma for several different reasons. It can be a symptom of a disease, or the result of an event such as a severe head injury, a metabolic problem, or a seizure, head injury being the most common. Other causes are diabetes, hemorrhage, shock, or the result of large amounts of morphine or alcohol, which is called a toxic coma.

Most comas last from two to four weeks; the chances of recovery—without brain damage—after more than three months is less than 10 percent. Comas do not all resemble a deep sleep; there are different stages of a coma, and the progress of recovery is measured by the patient's increasing awareness of surrounding stimuli. Patients may begin to make movements or sounds, and become agitated; they may even make reflexive motions that mimic waking activities.

Some coma victims fall into a persistent vegetative state: Normal bodily functions continue, but without the patient's awareness. Breathing, blood pressure, food intake, and elimination are normal, and this vegetative state can last for years, or even decades; most who do wake have suffered severe brain damage and do not ever recover completely.

If and when a person begins to emerge from a coma, he or she begins by reacting to different stimuli. Gaining consciousness is not instant, like in the movies: It may take several days or weeks. First awakening may last only a couple of minutes, to the frustration of family and friends. But in the following days, the patient may awaken for gradually increasing intervals.

Sometimes a coma is chemically induced by a doctor—usually after a head injury—to aid in medical treatment and recovery.

The Glasgow Coma Scale is used to assess the severity of a coma by measuring three components: eye opening response, verbal response, and motor response:

The Glasgow Coma Scale

EYE OPENING RESPONSE

    E1 = None;
    E2 = To pain
    E3 = To speech
    E4 = Spontaneous

VERBAL RESPONSE

    V1 = None
    V2 = Incomprehensible
    V3 = Inappropriate
    V4 = Confused
    V5 = Oriented

MOTOR RESPONSE

    M1 = None to pain
    M2 = Extension to pain (decerebrate posturing)
    M3 = Flexion to pain (decorticate posturing)
    M4 = Withdrawal to pain
    M5 = Purposeful movement/localized response to pain
    M6 = Obeys commands

A score of E4V5M6 indicates the normal state; a score of E1V1M1 indicates complete unresponsiveness.

TOP 10 REASONS TO STOP SMOKING

The National Heart, Lung, and Blood Institute suggests that anyone trying to give up cigarettes use these reminders of the benefits when the going gets difficult:

1. I will reduce my chances of having a heart attack or stroke.
2. I will reduce my chances of getting lung cancer, emphysema, and other lung diseases.
3. I will have better smelling clothes, hair, breath, home, and car.
4. I will climb stairs and walk without getting out of breath.
5. I will have fewer wrinkles.
6. I will be free of my morning cough.
7. I will reduce the number of coughs, colds, and earaches my child will have.
8. I will have more energy to pursue physical activities I enjoy.
9. I will treat myself to new books or music with the money I save from not buying cigarettes.
10. I will have more control over my life.

FRIEND OR FOE?

The handshake's origin was not so much a sign of greeting, but one of wary goodwill. Generally travelers who came upon each other on the road would draw their daggers with their right hand. When—and if—it became apparent that physical danger was not imminent, the daggers were sheathed and and the strangers would clasp hands as a sign of goodwill.

YES, THEY ARE WATCHING YOU

Part of the scariness of scary stories, camping, the woods, or just nature in general is the feeling you get at night that animals are skulking about, watching you. They can see you; you can't see them. In fact, every once in a while you get a glimpse—a pair of bright, yellow-green orbs, like mirrors, following you in the dark.

You're not imagining it. Wolves, raccoons, crocodiles—they all give off a sort of "eyeshine" from a mirror-like layer of cells in or behind the retina called the tapetum lucidum. Many nocturnal animals have it; the retina captures some of the light that enters the eye, but the rest of it passes through. The tapetum lucidum bounces it back to the retina, virtually giving the animal another chance to see, and making the animal's eyes essentially light up.

On a more domestic level, house cats are equipped with this kind of vision as well, allowing them 130 times better night vision than the human eye. The consolation? Humans have some of the best daytime vision in the animal kingdom.

'NIGHTY-'NIGHT!

Warm milk contains melatonin, a known sleep aid, and tryptophan, the ingredient in turkey that makes you doze off after Thanksgiving dinner—so it makes perfect sense that a glass may help you nod off at bedtime.

◆

The telephone AREA CODE in a portion of northeastern Florida that includes Cape Canaveral is 321. As in "3-2-1, LIFT-OFF!"

DREAM ON

It seems there are as many types of dreams as there are interpretations for them. Here are just a few of life's more common sleep stories, with the reasons why you dream them:

Animals: Of course it depends on the type of animal; dreaming about your pets or other domesticated animals may mean good fortune; wild animals denote fear and bad luck. Insects in general mean something in your waking life is nagging you.

Bed: An extremely common element in dreams (see HOUSE), and though Freud may call it the womb, it can denote a sexual encounter, sickness, or death.

Car: Also a very common object, symbolizing power, status, and sexuality. Generally it's about new life, but of course it depends on who's driving and what type of journey and car it is. Is it dangerous? Do you trust the person behind the wheel? Is it a long trip? Who's really in control?

Celebrities: Meeting a famous person in a dream may indicate a profitable offer is coming your way.

Chase: Running away is one of dreamdom's most frightening motifs, a response to threats in out waking lives. This is why so often we feel unable to move. But dreaming about being pursued may be a good way of coping with fears and stress. If, in your dream, you are caught by whoever is chasing you, you have a lot of work do to about the real-life problem; if you escape, you are nearly free.

Child: Especially if the child is an infant, this could be anxiety for men as much as it means wish-fulfillment for women;

either way, it's about great responsibilities.

Death: If the experience is a near-death event, it is often the result of a lucid dream, which occurs as the body is going to sleep. This dream is about a sense of vulnerability and of being out of control of the circumstances surrounding you.

If you do actually die in your dream, it can signify a release from current anxieties in your life, and point toward a rebirth that is about to occur.

Dreaming of the death of a loved one means you're feeling worried about their well-being.

Devils, Demons: If a demon helps you in your dream, it may signify the moral dilemma you feel about the task you've completed—a deal with the devil. If the demon is working against you, it could be you feel some evil—perhaps in the form of a person—is working against you in your waking life. If the demon threatens others, you may be worried about how to protect those important to you.

Exam: How many times have you had others tell you about having this dream? "I got to the class, and I realized I hadn't once opened the book/had never attended the class all semester, and here I was at the final!" Sometimes the test is in another language, time is running out, or you're late.

It's a self-esteem/self-confidence dream, and is indicative of feeling that you're not good enough or ill-prepared for what's coming your way. Though life is a constant test, this dream may stand for a particular approaching challenge you fear you can't meet.

Falling: It's an old wives' tale that you will die in your sleep if you hit the ground; there are many who have lived to tell the tale. Falling is the most common dream of all. You may *feel* like you want to check out; this dream indicates a sense of inferiority or fear of failure in school, work, finances, or love. These dreams often occur in the first stages of sleep, accompanied by muscle spasms in the arms, legs, or whole body; these sudden contractions are known as myoclonic jerks. Sigmund Freud said falling may indicate a desire to give in to an urge—perhaps an indiscreet one—sexual or of some other kind.

Fire: This is a common dream regardless of the dreamer's culture. It very often signifies purification, and passing through the flames in the dream is very positive. If you are burned, however, you perceive life as painful.

Flying: Flying dreams are lucid dreams, a category of dreams in which you become aware that you are dreaming. We think of flying as the ultimate freedom: If, in your dreams, it is exhilarating, joyful, and liberating, and you are enjoying the scenery below, you are feeling in control and on top of life. But if you are having difficulties staying in the air, and are fearful, you may be afraid of meeting challenges, out of control and afraid of success.

Food: Preparing or eating food means happiness and domestic contentment. Being hungry or thirsty often indicates spiritual dissatisfaction.

Garden: A lush garden in bloom means healthy growth of the soul; dead or weed-infested gardens mean you are aware of the need for spiritual growth.

House: It's generally a symbol of many things, and is second most common after falling as a dream motif. The house represents you, each room an aspect of your waking life. Doors may come as a complete surprise ("I've lived here forever and I never saw that!") and represent opportunities—sometimes scary ones—and should be opened.

Lost: Driving, shopping, and amusement parks often play a part; your opportunities are questionable and you feel you lack the ability to make the right choice. As in your waking life, you feel isolated, and that life is not progressing as you had hoped.

Naked: You're hiding something in your waking life, or feeling shameful. You're sure, in the dream, that everyone can see what a fraud you are, now that you're undressed before them. Many people see this with the exam dream.

Sexual: Sexual dreams are not unusual and can be extremely healthy if the emotions in the dream are not abnormal; it is not unusual to awake sexually aroused.

Teeth: In dreams they express your thoughts about your physical appearance and how others see you. Teeth can be power: They bite, tear, chew; conversely, losing them in your dream may indicate a feeling of powerlessness. Some cultures think dreaming of teeth signifies the death of someone close to you (the Chinese believe that your teeth fall out if you tell lies). There is also a theory that losing teeth symbolizes money, like our old friend the Tooth Fairy taught us.

Time: Dates and numbers may represent a time or event that is serving as the trigger for the dream.

Water: Again, as in life, so it is in dreams. Traditionally, calm water means good times ahead, clear sailing. Rough waters signify caution, and a warning to reconsider your course of action.

DOG GONE

The top reasons dogs are given up by their owners and brought to an animal shelter are behavioral. Unfortunately, pets often don't live up to their owners' unrealistic expectations: Chewing, hyperactivity, and soiling the house are often cited. Other reasons often given are:

- Moving from one's home
- Landlord prohibits pets
- Too many animals in the household
- Cost of veterinary care
- Owner's personal problems
- Inadequate facilities
- Aggression toward other pets
- Hostility toward other people

LUCK OF THE DRAW

In the Middle Ages, children and teenagers didn't send valentines to the other kids they had a crush on. They drew names from a bowl, and the name you picked was your special valentine for the entire week. They wore these slips of paper on their sleeves for all seven days; now we say you "wear your heart on your sleeve" when you make it obvious to everyone how you feel.

Some theorize that the tradition of throwing SALT over the left shoulder to ward off bad luck originates from Judas's having spilled salt at the Last Supper.

WHY, ROBOT

Author Isaac Asimov (1920–1992) devised the Three Rules of Robotics, which the robots in his books and short stories were obligated to follow. Many authors have adopted these rules for their fictional robots as well.

First Law: A robot may not harm a human being, or, through inaction, allow a human being to come to harm.

Second Law: A robot must obey the orders given to it by human beings, except where such orders would conflict with the First Law.

Third Law: A robot must protect its own existence, as long as such protection does not conflict with the First or Second Laws.

BIRD FEED

Why do chickens have white breast meat and dark thigh meat? Dare we ask if it has to do with chicken exercise? The muscles in constant use have high myoglobin content, which is caused by higher levels of oxygen and produces red muscle fiber, or dark meat. This is true of all fowl, including chicken, turkey, duck, and goose.

This also explains why fowl have white muscle tissue. White meat comes from the parts of a bird where muscles are less used and require less oxygen. Since neither chickens nor turkeys fly regularly, their chest muscles are used for bursts of speed on an as-needed basis, using glycogen as fuel instead of myoglobin. The less exercised meat looks white when cooked, and the more constantly used legs and wings appear dark.

BYE-BYE, LOVE?
Why and how people bury their dead like they do

Funerary customs are as old as death itself, and have grown out of fear, religion, gender, ignorance, and of course, love and respect. Most cultures have ceremonies, which often include a wake or other viewing of the deceased, a sacred place for the dead, and memorialization of the dead.

Some early burial rituals addressed the fear of the dead coming back to haunt the living and perhaps settle old scores; some believed they needed to protect themselves from whatever evil spirits had taken their beloved.

A few of the ways—some traditional or historic—people have said good-bye to their loved ones throughout time around the world:

- Some African tribes grind the bones of their dead and sprinkle them into their food.
- The Calatians ate their dead— it was not only the duty of the family, but an honor.
- Zulus burn the dead's belongings to drive spirits from the area.
- Cypriots visited a mummified relative as a family, changed the clothing of the dead, and had family chats with them.
- Hara kiri is an old Japanese death sacrifice, but upon the death of a nobleman, twenty or thirty slaves would commit suicide.
- A Hindu tradition, outlawed by the British, required *suttee*, or the immolation of a spouse, upon the death of a married man. The widow would dress her best, climb upon the funeral pyre, lie down next to her husband, and allow their eldest son to light the pyre. She would be cremated alive.

- On Bali, widow sacrifice was also common, with the women drugged and hypnotized before their cremation.
- At an Amish funeral, the number of mourners in attendance varies according to the deceased's age.
- Fear most likely underlies the custom of cremation; people burned the dead to destroy the evil spirits. Even today, some primitive tribes simply leave their dead to rot or be eaten by predators, while they flee the spirits left behind.
- Zororastrians also leave their dearly departed to the forces of nature. They believe fire is too sacred and that mother earth should not be defiled.
- The ringing of bells at a funeral service is a medieval carry-over; it was believed that evil spirits would never near a bell that had been blessed.
- Covering the face of the deceased originated not from concerns of privacy or discomfort about viewing the dead, but from pagan tribes who believed that the spirit of the dead escaped from the mouth. Mourners wore special clothing, believing them to be a disguise—they would trick any returning spirits from recognizing them.
- The Hindi may honor the dead by walking around the funeral pyre, but do not look at the flames; however, they are supposed to see to it that the skull bursts in the pyre, as the soul lives there and must be released.
- Hungarians put unchristened children, suicides, and murderers in boxes that are buried—without any services—in a churchyard trench.
- Often, men and women are treated differently in death: The Cochieans buried women and hung men from trees; Ghonds buried women and cremated men; and the Bongas buried men facing north, and women facing south.
- Feasts, wakes, parties, and memorials are remnants of offering food and drink to the deities.

THE UNWELL

The American Psychiatric Association defines a personality disorder as an enduring pattern of inner experience and behavior that:

- deviates markedly from the expectation of the individual's culture
- is pervasive and inflexible
- has an onset in adolescence or early adulthood
- is stable over time
- leads to distress or impairment

Types of Disorders

ANXIETY DISORDERS

Acute Stress Disorder: anxiety symptoms following recent exposure to trauma

Panic Disorder: short-term attacks of anxiety, often without warning

Agoraphobia without History of Panic Disorder: anxiety about leaving home and/or being in public places

Social Phobia: extreme anxiety in social situations

Specific Phobia (formerly Simple Phobia): an irrational fear of a situation or object

Obsessive-Compulsive Disorder: recurring unwanted thoughts or repeated actions

Post-Traumatic Stress Disorder: long-term anxiety resulting from a particularly traumatic event

Generalized Anxiety Disorder: excessive, frequent worry with no specific cause

CHILDHOOD DISORDERS

Attention-Deficit Hyperactivity Disorder: inability to concentrate or control impulses, most often in young people

Asperger's Syndrome: milder variant of autism

Autistic Disorder: lifelong developmental disability characterized by impaired communicative and interactive skills

Conduct Disorder: inappropriate, disruptive childhood behavior

Oppositional Defiant Disorder: long-term pattern of hostility, disobedience, et al toward authority figures

Separation Anxiety Disorder: excessive and inappropriate distress about separation from home or an individual

Tourette's Disorder: neurological disorder characterized by body or verbal tics

EATING DISORDERS

Anorexia Nervosa: characterized by mistaken belief one is overweight

Bulimia Nervosa: characterized by bingeing and vomiting

MOOD DISORDERS

Major Depressive Disorder: pattern of hopelessness, helplessness, worthlessness, thoughts of suicide

Bipolar Disorder (Manic Depression): characterized by alternating episodes of mania and depression

Cyclothymic Disorder: mild form of bipolar disorder

Dysthymic Disorder: long-term depressive disorder characterized by more days of feeling down than positive

COGNITIVE DISORDERS

Delirium: state of mental disturbance and agitation

Multi-Infarct Dementia: partial loss of brain function due to series of strokes

Dementia: the loss of intellectual function; causes may include alcoholism or Alzheimer's disease

Personality Disorders

Paranoid Personality Disorder: characterized by extreme distrust

Schizoid Personality Disorder: pattern of social isolation and indifference to others

Schizotypal Personality Disorder: mild form of bipolar disorder

Antisocial Personality Disorder: extreme disregard for feelings of others, obsession with personal gain

Borderline Personality Disorder: continual instability in personal relationships

Histrionic Personality Disorder: overdramatic reactions in unwarranted situations

Narcissistic Personality Disorder: inflated, unrealistic feelings of self-worth

Avoidant Personality Disorder: persons stay away from any chance of conflict

Dependent Personality Disorder: overreliance on others

Psychotic Disorders

Schizophrenia: general term for wide range of disassociative disorders

Delusional Disorder: consistent persecutory, jealous, grandiose feelings

Brief Psychotic Disorder: short-term episode brought on by stressful events

Schizophreniform Disorder: short-term schizophrenic episode characterized by hallucinations and delusions

Schizoaffective Disorder: marked by both schizophrenic and manic-depressive symptoms

Shared Psychotic Disorder: a system that develops in two or more extremely close persons, one of whom is delusional

Depressive Disorders
Depression: characterized by feelings of inadequacy and inertia
Major Depressive Episode: loss of interest in almost all
   activities for at least two weeks
Dysthymia: chronic and mild depression
Seasonal Affective Disorder: depression during fall and winter
Postnatal Depression: sadness in the days and weeks after
   giving birth, often leading to inability to care for child

Substance-Related Disorders
These include dependence on alcohol, drugs (cocaine,
   amphetamines, marijuana, opiates, sedatives, hallu-
   cinogens, or inhalants), or nicotine.

◆

COLOR MY WORLD

Chromotherapists use color combined with light to balance a
person's energy in their physical, spiritual, emotional and
mental capacities:

   RED—awakens both physical and mental energies
   ORANGE—beneficial for the solar plexus and the lungs
   YELLOW—stimulates the nerves
   BLUE—heals organic disorders like colds, allergies and
   liver problems
   GREEN—alleviates stress
   INDIGO—acts on fever and skin problems

◆

Metal atoms in the red pigment of HEMOGLOBIN can
carry the large quantities of oxygen humans and other large
vertebrates require.

THE STATE OF YOUR ESTATE

Lawyers say that these are some of the most common reasons people should do their estate planning in advance:

1. To designate an executor and someone who will manage your affairs should you become disabled or pass away.
2. To assure that your estate remains sound should you need to go to a nursing home or assisted living facility.
3. To avoid probate, during your life and after.
4. To protect children from a prior marriage should you pass away first.
5. To protect your heirs from lawsuits and similar claims, such as those arising from divorce.
6. To help children and grandchildren who have no experience managing money, or who may have special needs.
7. To insure that specific monies or gifts from your estate go to the people, institutions, and charities you wish.
8. To protect your estate for the rest of your family in case you predecease a spouse who remarries.
9. To care for the different needs of different children.
10. To prevent challenges to your estate.
11. To reward or encourage heirs who make wise life decisions, and prevent the depletion of the estate by those who may not.
12. To set aside money for childrens' and/or grandchildrens' education, regardless of the wishes of their parents.
13. To assure a new stepparent doesn't spend your children's inheritance.
14. To be sure that the portion of your estate meant for your spouse does not go to his/her new spouse and that spouse's family.

THANKS, WALT

After audiences' delighted response to Walt Disney's first full-length animated film, *Snow White and the Seven Dwarves*, the studio knew it had a good thing going. It started a long history of animated successes, including:

Fantasia (1940)
Pinocchio (1940)
Dumbo (1941)
Bambi (1942)
The Adventures of Ichabod and Mr. Toad (1949)
Cinderella (1950)
Peter Pan (1953)
Lady and the Tramp (1955)
Sleeping Beauty (1959)
101 Dalmations (1961)
The Aristocats (1970)
Robin Hood (1973)
The Many Adventures of Winnie the Pooh (1977)
The Fox and the Hound (1981)
The Great Mouse Detective (1986)
The Little Mermaid (1989)
Beauty and the Beast (1991)
Aladdin (1992)
The Lion King (1994)
Pocahontas (1995)
The Hunchback of Notre Dame (1996)
Mulan (1998)
Tarzan (1999)
The Emperor's New Groove (2000)
Lilo & Stitch (2002)

ALWAYS GREENER
Why is there such lawn envy?

Until the Industrial Revolution, only the wealthy were lucky
enough to have manicured lawns. English gardens and lawns
had long been the envy of homeowners around the world,
but either one had a staff of men with scythes or, as both
George Washington and Thomas Jefferson had, a flock of
sheep on the front lawn, keeping things trim.

Early in the nineteenth century, an Englishman named
Edwin Budding developed a lawn mower, which he designed
after a machine that sheared the nap on velvet. In 1870,
Elwood McGuire improved on it, and fifteen years later,
Americans were buying 50,000 lawnmowers a year. Still, the
lawns didn't look like those across the pond.

The American Garden Club sponsored contests and
worked to persuade homeowners that a beautiful lawn and
was a public duty. Meanwhile, the U.S. Department of
Agriculture and U.S. Golf Association joined forces in 1915
to concoct the right combination of grasses for both a beautiful fairway and a gorgeous backyard. Pesticides and herbi-
cides were now in the increasingly expensive picture.

Though few countries in the world have the dewy, tem-
perate climate that makes the English garden possible, they
continue to try. In the United States alone, homeowners
spend $17 billion on outdoor improvements, and more than
26 million households hire professionals to help with their
yard work, landscaping, and gardening.

Recently, however, environmentalists have criticized the
plethora of manicured lawns for many reasons:

• Single species plants reduce biodiversity, and local biodiversity suffers when plants are imported simply for
  reasons of beautification.

- Pesticides (over 136 million pounds in 1997) and other chemicals often do environmental damage; 99 percent of urban stream samples tested positive for pesticides in 1999.
- Use of water for lawns in climates that don't normally support grass puts strain on local water supplies; 30 to 60 percent of it is urban fresh water.
- A gas lawn mower pollutes as much in one hour as a car does in 350 miles.
- An acre of wetland or prairie costs $150 a year to maintain; an acre of lawn, approximately $1,000; there are more than 20 million acres of lawn in the United States—more than any other single crop in the country.

SPACE HEROES

A Short Calculation of Those Who Have Given Their Lives for Science

3	*Apollo 1* (US)
1	*Soyuz 1* (USSR)
3	*Soyuz 11* (USSR)
7	*Challenger* space shuttle (US)
7	*Columbia* space shuttle (US)
50	Plesetsk launchpad employees (USSR)
71	Total

One's NAME DAY is the feast of a (usually lesser known) saint bearing your first name. Sometimes there is more than one saint with the same name and hence multiple name days: for example, the name day for Rebecca is either March 23 or July 19, and the name day for Philippa is either February 27 or May 7.

TO YOU!
Why and how we lift a glass around the globe

Toasts began as thanks and a prayer to the gods before a feast. Perhaps this is why we still refer to liquor as "nectar of the gods." Here are some toasts from around the world:

Albania	*Gezuar*
Armenia	*Genatzt*
Austria	*Prosit*
Azerbijan	*Noosh Olsum*
Bali	*Selamat*
Belgium	*Op Uw Gezonheid*
Brazil	*Saude*
Burma	*Auug Bar See*
China	*Wen Lei*
China	*Yam Sing (Cantonese)*
China	*Ganbei (Mandarin)*
Croatia	*Na Zdravlje*
Denmark	*Skaal*
Egypt	*Fee Sihetak*
England	*Cheers*
Estonia	*Tervist*
Ethiopia	*Letenatchie*
Finland	*Kippis*
France	*A Votre Sante*
Germany	*Prosit*
Georgia (Republic)	*Gaumardjos*
Greece	*Iss Ighian*
Greenland	*Kasugta*
Hawaii	*Okele Maluna*
Hawaii	*Hauoli Maoli Oe*
Holland	*Proost*

Hungary	*Kedves Egeszsegere*
Iceland	*Samtaka Nu*
India	*Aancllld*
Indonesia	*Selamat*
Ireland	*Slainte*
Israel	*Le Chaim*
Italy	*Alla Tua Salute*
Italy	*Per cent'anni!*
Japan	*Kampai*
Japan	*Banzai*
Korea	*Kong Gang Ul Wi-Ha Yo*
Kyrgyzstan	*Den Sooluck Yuchun*
Latvia	*Lai ta Buda Ruc*
Latvia	*Prieka*
Latvia	*Uz Veselibu*
Lebanon	*Vesar*
Lithuania	*I Sveikata*
Malaysia	*Yam Seng*
Malaya	*Slamat Minum*
Mexico	*Salud*
Morocco	*Saha Wa Afiab*
New Zealand	*Kia-Ora*
Norway	*Skaal*
Old English	*Wes Thu Hale*
Pakistan	*Zanda Bashi*
Persia (Iran)	*Salaamati*
Phillipines	*Mabuhay*
Poland	*Na Zdrowie*
Portugal	*A Sua Saude*
Romania	*Noroc*
Romania	*Sanatatee*
Romania	*Dumneavoastrua*
Russia	*Za Vashe Zdorovia*

Scotland	*Shlante*
Slovak	*Nazdravie*
South Africa	*Gesondheid*
Spain	*Salud*
Sudan	*Sabatuk Fy*
Swahili	*Afya*
Sweden	*Skäl*
Syria	*Kull Sana Wo*
Syria	*Enta Salem*
Tagalog	*Mubuhcly*
Tanzania	*Kwa Afya Yako*
Thailand	*Sawasdi*
Thailand	*Chai-o*
Tibet	*Tashidelek*
Tibet	*Phun Tsun Tsok*
Turkey	*Sherefe*
Ukraine	*Budjmo*
Ukraine	*Na Zdorovya*
Wales	*Lechyd da*
Yugoslavia	*Na Zdraviye*
Zulu	*Oogy Wawa*
Zulu	*Poo-zim-pee-La*

As a last word, the Swedish *skäl* means "drinking vessel," and is derived from the word for skull—which is exactly what the Swedes used to drink from.

◆

The PANAMA CANAL has two parallel sets of locks so that vessels may pass through the canal in both directions simultaneously. The lock chambers are 1,000 feet long, 110 feet wide, and 40 feet deep.

AND THE AWARD GOES TO . . .
Academy Award–winning movies that go by their own name

REAL FOLKS

The Great Ziegfeld (1936)
The Life of Emile Zola (1937)
Lawrence of Arabia (1962)
Patton (1970)
Gandhi (1982)
Amadeus (1984)
Schindler's List (1993)
Braveheart (1995)

AND FICTIONAL ONES

Rebecca (1940)
Mrs. Miniver (1942)
Hamlet (1948)
All About Eve (1950)
Marty (1955)
Gigi (1958)
Ben-Hur (1959)
Tom Jones (1963)
Oliver! (1968)
The Godfather (1972)
The Godfather, Part II (1974)
Rocky (1976)
Annie Hall (1977)
Kramer vs. Kramer (1979)
Driving Miss Daisy (1989)
Forrest Gump (1994)

HE LOOKS AWFULLY SUSPICIOUS

The FBI often look at suspects based on their sociopsychological profile when searching for serial killers:

Disorganized, Nonsocial Offenders	Organized, Asocial Offenders
IQ below average, 80–95	IQ above average, 105–120
Socially inadequate	Socially adequate
Lives alone, usually does not date	Lives with partner or dates frequently
Absent or unstable father	Stable father figure
Family emotional abuse, inconsistent	Family physical abuse, harsh
Lives and/or works near crime scene	Geographically and occupationally mobile
Minimal interest in news	Follows the news
Usually a high school dropout	May be college educated
Poor hygiene/housekeeping	Good hygiene/housekeeping
Keeps a secret hiding place in the home	Does not usually keep a hiding place
Nocturnal (nighttime) habits	Diurnal (daytime) habits
Drives a clunky car or pickup	Drives a flashy car
Returns to crime scene to relive memories	Returns to crime scene to see what police have done
Usually leaves body intact	May dismember body

Disorganized, Nonsocial Offenders	Organized, Asocial Offenders
May contact victim's family to play games	Usually contacts police to play games
No interest in police work	Police groupie or wannabe
Experiments with self-help programs	Doesn't experiment with self-help
Kills at one site, considers mission over	Kills at one site, disposes at another
Attacks in a "blitz" pattern	Attacks using seduction into restraints
Depersonalizes victim	Personalizes, holds a conversation
Leaves a chaotic crime scene	Leaves a controlled crime scene
Leaves physical evidence	Leaves little physical evidence
Responds best to counseling interview	Responds best to direct interview

THE SCOTTISH PLAY

Traditionally, actors don't mention the name of Shakespeare's *Macbeth*. There are various theories about the source of the superstition: the witches' incantation in the play is said to be real; during an early performance, the actor playing Lady Macbeth, Hal Berridge, is thought to have died backstage; it's often performed when a theater company is in trouble because it's a box office winner.

"WHY DIDN'T I ORDER THE HOMARINE SALAD?"

Probably because you didn't know "homarine" was the adjective for lobster. Some other animal adjectives:

MAMMALS

Anteater	myrmecophagine
Antelope	bubaline
Ape	simian
Armadillo	tolypeutine
Ass	asinine
Auk	alcidine
Badger	musteline
Bear	ursine
Calf	vituline
Cat	feline
Cow	bovine
Deer	cervine
Dog	canine
Fox	vulpine
Goat	caprine
Hamster	cricetine
Leopard	pardine
Leo	lionine
Mouse	murine
Otter	lutrine
Pig	porcine
Porcupine	hystricine
Rabbit	leporine
Rhinoceros	ceratorhine
Ram	arietine

Sable	zabeline
Sheep	ovine
Shrew	soricine
Skunk	mephitine
Squirrel	sciurine
Tiger	tigrine
Whale	cetacean
Wolf	lupine
Zebra	zebrine

BIRDS

Blackbird	icterine
Bluebird	turdine
Buzzard	beuteonine
Cormorant	phalacrocoracine
Crow	corvine
Cuckoo	cuculine
Dod	didine
Dove	columbine
Duck	anatine
Eagle	aqualine
Falcon	accipitrine
Goose	anserine
Gull	larine
Jay	garruline
Ostrich	struthionine
Owl	strigine
Peacock	pavonine
Quail	coturnine
Sparrow	passerine
Stork	ciconine
Swan	cygnine

| Turkey | meleagrine |
| Wren | troglodytine |

FISH

Barracuda	percesocine
Dolphin	delphine
Fish	piscine

INSECTS

Ant	formicine
Bee	apian
Flea	pulicine
Mosquito	aedine
Moth	arctian
Wasp	vespine

MARSUPIAL

| Kangaroo | macropodine |

REPTILES

| Alligator | eusuchian |
| Rattlesnake | crotoline |

◆

New Orleans JAZZ owes some of its roots to military marching bands. When a band was (pardon the expression) disbanded as impractical to modern warfare at a military base in Louisiana, many of the instruments were repurposed by local musicians, who adapted them to their own musical style.

HOGGING THE TRUFFLES

Often one hears of a truffle-hunting pig, specially trained to ferret out the world's best, most prized and hard-to-find mushrooms. In the United States, most truffles are found in in Oregon and Washington, states whose weather and topography are similar to the truffle-rich parts France and Italy. In Europe, truffle hunters use pigs and mixed-breed dogs for hunting—the dogs are preferred because the pigs enjoy a truffle as much as a human, and are as likely to eat them as find them. A truffle hunter will often carry a staff to force the pig away from the prize.

Dogs are the better bet, because they prefer other foods besides mushrooms. The hunter brings treats for the dog, who is not fed the night before; he is not eager to eat a truffle, but he knows finding one will earn him a reward.

PLANE MAGIC

The first American air shows began around 1910. Realizing that this new, exciting form of transportation had grabbed people's imaginations, small groups of pilots banded together and put on shows to promote aviation, entertain, or simply to make a living. Where daredevils and large egos meet, competition is not far behind, and contests for highest, fastest, and best stunt performances became a popular new type of entertainment. Families came to the airfields on the outskirts of town, picnics and all, and made a day of it. By the beginning of World War I, air shows had become a worldwide phenomenon. The United States was a bit behind: The first international air show took place in Reims, France in August 1909—with nearly 500,000 spectators.

WHAT ARE YOU TRYING TO SAY?

When you see symbols like this on your computer screen, you can be sure someone is saying *exactly* what they mean. Whether you find them annoying or adorable, these symbols are certainly universal. They're called emoticons, and they're the "flower-dotted i" of the computer age. Herewith enough for a short novel:

:-) or :)	Smile
:-D or :d	Open-mouthed
:-O or :o	Surprised
:-P or :p	Tongue out
;-) or ;)	Wink
:-(or :(	Sad
:-S or :s	Confused
:-| or :|	Disappointed
:'(	Crying
:-$ or :$	Embarrassed
(H) or (h)	Hot
:-@ or :@	Angry
(A) or (a)	Angel
(6)	Devil
:-#	Don't tell anyone
8o|	Baring teeth
8-|	Nerd
^o)	Sarcastic
:-*	Secret telling
+o(	Sick
:^)	I don't know
*-)	Thinking
<:o)	Party

8-)	Eye rolling
|-)	Sleepy
!-)	Proud of black eye
#-)	Wiped out; partied all night
#:-o	Shocked
$-)	Won the lottery; money on the brain
%-(	Confused
%-)	Dazed or silly
%-\	Hung over
%-|	Worked all night
%-}	Humorous or ironic
>-	Female
>-)	Devilish wink
>:)	Little devil
>:-<	Angry
>:-(	Annoyed
>:-)	Mischievous devil
<:->	Devilish expression
<:-(	Dunce
<:-)	Innocently asking dumb question
(8(|)	Homer
(<> .. <>)	Alienated
()	Hugging
(-:	Left-handed smile; smiley from southern hemisphere
(:-&	Angry
(:-(	Unsmiley
(:-*	Kiss
(:-\	Very sad
(::():::)	Bandaid, meaning comfort
(:|	Egghead
*	Kiss
*<:-)	Santa Claus

+<:-|	Monk or nun
+<||-)	Knight
+:-)	Priest
+O:-)	The Pope
-)	Tongue in cheek
-=	Snuffed candle to end a flame message
/\/\/\	Laughter
0:-)	Angel
2B|^2B	To be or not to be
5:-)	Elvis
8	Infinity
8 :-)	Wizard
8-#	Death
8-o	Shocked
8-O	Astonished
8-P	Yuck!
8-[	Frayed nerves; overwrought
8-]	Wow!
8-|	Wide-eyed surprise
: (	Sad
:)	Smile
: [	Bored, sad
:( )	Loudmouth; talks all the time;
:*	Kiss
:*)	Clowning
:**:	Returning kiss
:+(	Got punched in the nose
:,(	Crying
:-	Male
:-#	My lips are sealed; wearing braces
:-&	Tongue-tied
:->	Smile of happiness or sarcasm
:-><	Puckered up to kiss

:-<	Very sad
:-,	Smirk
:-/	Wry face
:-6	Exhausted
:-9	Licking lips
:-?	Licking lips; tongue in cheek
:-@	Screaming
:-C	Astonished
:-c	Very unhappy
:-D	Laughing
:-d~	Heavy smoker
:-e	Disappointed
:-f	Sticking out tongue
:-I	Pondering; impartial
:-i	Wry smile or half-smile
:-J	Tongue in cheek
:-l	One-sided smile
:-M	Speak no evil
:-o	Surprised look; yawn
]:->	Devil
]:-)	Happy devil
][	Back to back

♦

RISING TO THE OCCASION

Yeast does double duty: It makes bread rise and it makes
alcoholic beverages ferment. Yeasts are single-celled fungi
that produce energy by converting sugars to carbon dioxide
and ethanol. In bread, the carbon dioxide makes the dough
rise (the ethanol evaporates); in beer, the ethanol is captured
in the bottle. Saccharomyces cerevisiae is the most commonly used type of yeast.

WAS IT AN INCREDIBLY
BUMPY SILK ROAD?
And why some silks are not so smooth

Silk was supposedly discovered by accident: Yuen Fei, a Chinese emperor's concubine, accidently dropped a cocoon into her tea, whereupon it unraveled, and the thread attracted sufficient attention to become a luxury fabric.

The gathering and waving of silk remained secret processes—some say for nearly thirty centuries, until Japan discovered it around 300 B.C.E. By that time, silk had become such a valuable commodity that it was often traded for luxuries from Europe. It is said that Julius Caesar allowed no one else in the Roman empire to wear silk but himself. Until the sixth century, silk came entirely from Asia, until Emperor Justinian I sent monks undercover to steal mulberry seeds and silkworm eggs and hide them in their staffs and bring silk to Europe.

Only a few moths (after their lives as caterpillars) are used to produce silk, the mulberry silk moth, *Bombyx mori*, being the most common. Herewith a few fascinating facts, from worm to weave:

- One ounce of eggs produces about 20,000 worms; they will consume about one ton of mulberry leaves before they die.
- Tusah silk is produced by silkworms that feed on oak, not mulberry, leaves.
- 5,500 silkworms will produce only 2¼ pounds of raw silk.
- The very popular dupioni, or shantung, silk is produced from two silkworms spinning a cocoon together. In weaving, the double strand is not separated, and the uneven, irregular feel has become its hallmark.

TOWER OF FAITH

The flying buttress made an amazing difference in the architectural beauty of cathedrals when the Gothic era, with its increased knowledge of engineering, arrived in the eleventh century. Along with other features such as ribbed vaults, steeply pointed spires and arches, the design allowed much more space for the advent of huge and numerous stained glass windows, and therefore increased natural light. The flying buttress was the key to this more open and gracious structure; it allowed for higher ceilings, and most importantly, the buttress carried the weight of roofs that were heavier than the roofs common in the churches that came before.

HURRY SUNDOWN?

Though most of the world uses daylight saving time, there is some opposition to the idea.

Farmers, for whom an extra hour of sunlight would seem to be a boon, often say that it's all right with them, but not so much with the animals. Chickens and cows take several weeks to get used to the new time, making the farmers' routines difficult. And Orthodox Sephardic Jews have issues around the dark mornings during the month of Elul, when penitential prayers are recited.

There is a benefit to the time change that can't be denied: the number of traffic accidents and fatalities decrease in the United States and the United Kingdom by nearly one percent by virtue of having more light later at night, when drivers tend to have more accidents.

WORDS TO WRITE BY

The Turkey City Lexicon is a set of terms that writers use as shorthand to describe certain types of flaws in each other's prose. It was compiled by authors Lewis Shiner and Bruce Sterling. Some examples:

Brenda Starr Dialogue: Long sections of talk with no physical background or description of the characters. Such dialogue, detached from the story's setting, tends to echo hollowly, as if suspended in mid-air. Named for the American comic-strip in which dialogue balloons were often seen emerging from the Manhattan skyline.

"Burly Detective" Syndrome: The hack writers of the Mike Shayne series showed an odd reluctance to use Shayne's proper name, preferring such euphemisms as "the burly detective" or "the red-headed sleuth." This syndrome arises from a wrong-headed conviction that the same word should not be used twice in close succession.

Brand Name Fever: Use of brand name alone, without accompanying visual detail, to create false verisimilitude.

Gingerbread: Useless ornament in prose, such as fancy sesquipedalian Latinate words where short clear English ones will do.

Not Simultaneous: The misuse of the present participle is a common structural sentence-fault for beginning writers. "Putting his key in the door, he leapt up the stairs and got his revolver out of the bureau." Alas, our hero couldn't do this even if his arms were forty feet long.

Pushbutton Words: Words used to evoke a cheap emotional response without engaging the intellect or the critical faculties. Commonly found in story titles, they include such bits of bogus lyricism as "star," "dance," "dream," "song," "tears," and "poet," calculated to render the audience misty-eyed and tender-hearted.

Roget's Disease: The ludicrous overuse of far-fetched adjectives, piled into a festering, fungal, tenebrous, troglodytic, ichorous, leprous, synonymic heap.

"Said" Bookism: An artificial verb used to avoid the word "said." The term "said-book" comes from certain pamphlets, containing hundreds of purple-prose synonyms for the word "said," which were sold to aspiring authors from tiny ads in American magazines of the era before World War II.

Tom Swifty: A compulsion to follow the word "said" with a colorful adverb, as in "'We'd better hurry,' Tom said swiftly." This was a standard mannerism of the old Tom Swift adventure dime-novels.

Countersinking: A form of expositional redundancy in which the action clearly implied in dialogue is made explicit. "'Let's get out of here,' he said, urging her to leave."

Dischism: The unwitting intrusion of the author's physical surroundings, or the author's own mental state, into the text of the story. Authors who smoke or drink while writing often drown or choke their characters with an endless supply of booze and cigs. "Dischism" is named after Thomas M. Disch, who first diagnosed this syndrome.

False Interiorization: A cheap labor-saving technique in which the author, too lazy to describe the surroundings, afflicts the viewpoint-character with a blindfold, an attack of space-sickness, the urge to play marathon whist-games in the smoking-room, etc.

Fuzz: An element of motivation the author was too lazy to supply. The word "somehow" is a useful tip-off to fuzzy areas of a story. "Somehow she had forgotten to bring her gun."

WHY CAN'T I GET THE BLUE PLATE SPECIAL?

Because it's been "86ed"—and other tidbits of diner slang

Like so much slang, its etymology is lost in time; though with diner slang, there appears to be some proof that as far back as the 1870s, black waiters were using at least some of the phrases listed here. One thing's for sure: it's all based in good fun, made up to lighten the mood in stressful environments. Listen closely next time you sit down at a lunch counter, and see if you can spot your order.

Numbers Slang:

41 = lemonade
51 = hot chocolate
55 = root beer
86 = the kitchen is out of it, or, cancel the order
95 = customer jumping the check
99 = report to the manager

Eggs:

Adam and Eve on a raft = poached eggs on toast
deadeye = poached egg
wreck 'em = scrambled eggs
Fry two, let the sun shine = 2 fried eggs with unbroken yolk

Meat:

first lady = spare ribs (another Adam and Eve reference)
Pittsburgh = rare meat, cold in the middle, charred on the outside
on the hoof = meat cooked rare

Noah's boy = ham (Ham was Noah's second son)
groundhog, bow wow, Coney Island = hot dog
burn one, clean up the kitchen = hamburger
two cows, make 'em cry = two burgers with onions
hockey puck = hamburger, well done
take a chance = hash
bowl of red = chili
Irish turkey = corn beef and cabbage
radio = tuna (like saying "tuna" or "turn it down")
Bossy in a bowl = beef stew
zeppelin = sausage

Drinks:

city, city juice, 81, dog soup = water
moo juice, cow, 5 = milk
java, joe, draw one = coffee
pair of drawers = two coffees
an M.D. = a Dr. Pepper
blonde and sweet = coffee with milk and sugar
sinkers and suds, life preservers = doughnuts and coffee
squeeze one = orange juice
creep = draft beer

Desserts:

fish eyes = tapioca pudding
bucket of mud = bowl of chocolate ice cream
houseboat = banana split
nervous pudding = Jello
Eve with the lid on = apple pie

Staff and surroundings:

bubble dancer = dishwasher

gallery = booth
lumber = toothpick
soup jockey = waitress

Other:

sand, yum-yum = sugar
twins, Mike and Ike = salt and pepper
burn the British = English muffin, toasted
birdseed = bowl of cereal
hail = ice
shingle with a shimmy = toast with jelly
blowout patches = pancakes
machine oil = syrup
rabbit food = lettuce
keep off the grass = no lettuce
pin a rose on it = with onions
Frog sticks = French fries
A Murphy = a potato
cut the grass = no relish (on a hot dog or hamburger)
paint it red = with ketchup
sea dust = salt
warts = olives
put a hat on it = add ice cream
boiled leaves = tea
a spot with a twist= a cup of tea with lemon
in the alley = served on the side
high and dry = served plain
a million on a platter = a plate of baked beans
crowd = three of anything (as in "Two's company . . .")
on wheels, take it for a walk = order to go
whiskey = rye bread (as in rye whiskey)
dog biscuit = cracker

MAGIC METAL
The amazing new world of "memory metal"

A certain alloy made of nickel and titanium has changed the, well, shape of metallurgy. It's called memory metal, and its special shape memory effect, or SME, makes it possible for objects to be deformed, and then subsequently retain, their original shape.

The metal can be twisted and reshaped in any way, then reheated and brought back to "square one" at a certain temperature. This memory metal's crystal structure is transformed, but not destroyed; heating causes the atoms to reassume their original order. There are two types of "memory": a one-way SME can be changed, then recover its original shape when heated. A two-way alloy holds its first-position shape at one temperature, and can take on a completely new shape when heated at another temperature.

NASA began to explore this technology in the 1960s, and finally employed it in building the space station in the 1980s. At that point, commercial adaptations were beginning to appear, and home and industrial products hit the market. One of the most astounding innovations is a tube made of this special alloy which is crushed and inserted into clogged blood vessels. The metal has a memory transfer temperature that is very close to the body temperature of a human, so that the tube will expand once inside, and open the clogged arteries.

Some other devices that have benefited from this technological advance:

- Antennas for mobile phones
- Spectacle frames
- Medical guide wires and tools

- Stents for vascular and nonvascular surgery
- Staples and plates for the repair of fractured bones
- Orthodontic archwires
- Fire security and protection devices
- Motor protectors
- Security door locks
- Heating and ventilation controls
- Food cooking safety indicators
- Steam vent controls

FAMILY OF CAT

Unspayed adult female cats remain in heat for about five days, and may mate with more than one male during that time. The litter (born about two months later) may include the offspring of more than one father, so the kittens may not look at all alike.

But you might not be able to tell how different at the outset. The kittens are not always born with their markings. Those develop over weeks: blue Persians, for example, are born with tabby-like markings. Eye colors change, too, from blue to the more common green or gold.

LAST WORDS

"I have six honest serving men
(They taught me all I knew);
Their names are What and Why and When
And How and Where and Who."

—Rudyard Kipling, *The Elephant's Child*